The Cook's Handbook

The Cook's Handbook

Fingertip Facts on Food and Cookery

Wendy Majerowicz
and Patricia Bourne

OCTOPUS

Contents

First published in 1980 by
Octopus Books Limited
59 Grosvenor Street, London W1
This edition published in 1983 by
Octopus Books Limited
59 Grosvenor Street, London W1

ISBN 0 7064 1803 4
Made and printed in Great Britain by
Richard Clay (The Chaucer Press) Limited
Bungay, Suffolk

Kitchencraft

Take a sharp knife.

Equipping a kitchen takes time and money. If you are setting up home for the first time, buy a few essentials first then add to these as you need and can afford to. Whether you are a novice or an experienced cook, always remember that a piece of equipment or a kitchen tool is only worth the money if you make full use of it.

Tools for the kitchen

With such a wide range of equipment now available, it is worth asking yourself when shopping, 'Will it do the job?' and 'Will I use it?'.

Value for money, durability and easy cleaning are also important, so here are a few suggestions to help you make the right choice.

Knives

Buy the best you can afford, good quality knives will last a lifetime. A knife must feel comfortable to work with, so pick each one up and make sure that the blade and handle balance evenly in your hand. Knives must be kept sharp; you are more likely to cut yourself on a blunt one as, instead of slicing through the food, it can slide off and cut your fingers. Choose a knife with a fine cutting edge as it will be easier to keep sharp. For this you will need a good *steel* (about 21 cm/8½ inches long). A steel will give a better edge than other types of sharpeners.

Buy a small *vegetable knife* for peeling and preparing vegetables, and a larger *cook's knife* with a firm blade for cutting and chopping.

An 18 cm/7½ inch knife should be large enough and heavy enough for all your tasks. A small *serrated-edged knife* is ideal for peeling and cutting fruit. You will need a *palette knife* for spreading, a *carving knife* and a *bread knife*. A *grapefruit knife*, with a curved blade serrated on both sides, can be useful. A good *vegetable peeler* will save you time and be more economical to use for peeling vegetables than a knife. Choose a swivel or fixed blade, whichever you prefer. A thin bladed *filleting knife* and a *boning knife*, with a short rigid blade, will be a great help if you do a lot of food preparation.

Stainless steel knives are easy to keep clean but if you want a filleting knife with a more flexible blade, you may be happier with one made from carbon steel. The disadvantage of this metal is that it stains easily, so clean well with a wire wool soap pad each time you use it. If it is not used often, rub a little oil over the blade before putting away, to prevent rusting.

Saucepans

These can also last a lifetime, so it is worth taking the time to make the right choice. Pans must heat evenly if they are to cook food evenly. They should have firm bases which won't buckle. Handles must be strong and firmly fixed, and be the right shape to hold and grip easily. Large pans should have a handle each side for safety. Check that the handles and any metal fittings will not burn you when you lift the pan. The balance of the pan in the hand is important. If it is too heavy when it is empty, imagine how unsafe it will be when full. Check that lids are well fitting but can be removed without sticking.

For most families, a *milk saucepan* with a lip for easy pouring and a set of 3 saucepans in graduated sizes will be sufficient. If you have a large family or do a great deal of cooking, you may like to have 1 or 2 large pans. If you make your own jams and pickles, then a *preserving pan* will be useful.

Enamel pans look pretty but make certain you buy good quality. Cheap ones will chip and because they are thin, food can easily burn in them.

Aluminium pans may not look so glamorous but when considering value for money, they are an excellent buy. They have the advantage over most other types of pans because they conduct heat evenly, therefore, food is less likely to burn on the bottom or sides of the pan. Buy ground base pans for electric and solid top cookers, as the bottom of the pans must be flat to make contact with the hot plate. This is not essential when cooking with gas, but flat bases which won't wobble are a safety asset.

Non-stick linings to saucepans take a lot of the hard work out of washing-up. They are continually being improved and some manufacturers claim they are virtually non-scratch, and that metal tools and cleaners can be used in them. Most still need careful handling and only plastic tools and non-scratch cleaners should be used. At least one non-stick pan for scrambling eggs, making custard, etc. is a great help.

Stainless steel pans look good, they are easy to clean and will not affect the flavour and colour of food such as wine sauces. Unfortunately, stainless steel is a poor conductor of heat. Although the best pans have aluminium sandwich or copper bases which protect the food in the bottom of the pan, it is liable to burn on the sides where the contents splash above the liquid line.

Copper pans look very attractive. Copper is also the most effective conductor of heat, and cooks evenly. However, there are snags. To keep the pans looking their best, they must be polished regularly. Domestic pans must be lined with tin, the tinning eventually wears away and must be renewed from time to time. Never cook acid foods such as rhubarb in unlined pans, or in any where the tinning has worn away, as the acid could react against the copper and cause poisoning. Copper pans also have the disadvantages of being heavy to use and expensive to buy.

Glass and ceramic pans also look attractive and are easy to clean, but ceramic heats unevenly. Their main disadvantage is that they don't bounce if dropped or knocked and, of course, glass will shatter if allowed to boil dry.

Frying pans

The choice of metals is similar to saucepans although cast iron frying pans are more easily available than saucepans. Cast iron is an excellent conductor of heat, it is heavy to use but is ideal for cooking omelettes and pancakes.

To make the best of your skills as a cook, you must keep one pan for omelettes. It can also be used for pancakes, although you may like a special low sided pancake or crêpe pan. Never wash either of these pans once they have been used because you will destroy the patina which builds up on the surface, and your omelettes and pancakes will stick. Season the pan before you use it. To do this, pour some oil on to the base and heat until very hot. Take off the heat and leave the oil in the pan overnight. Pour the oil out the next day, wipe the pan with kitchen paper and it is ready to use. If necessary, when you use it again, clean by putting a little salt into the pan. Heat through, shaking the pan until the salt runs freely and does not stick. Throw the salt away, wipe the pan with paper and then heat a little oil in the bottom before use.

Buy another general purpose frying pan; one with a lid can be useful. If buying an aluminium pan, choose a ground base one, as thinner frying pans buckle easily. You may also want a deep-frying pan with a basket.

Casseroles

You will certainly need 1 or 2 casseroles, the size and number will depend on your family or how much cooking you do.

There is a wide range from good plain earthenware to pretty enamel casseroles.

You may prefer flameproof ones which can be used on top of the cooker as well as in the oven. Most of the pretty ones are *enamel on steel.* They are hard wearing and durable but because they are thin, care must be taken that the food does not burn when used on top of the cooker. *Enamel on cast iron* are very heavy pans and conduct heat well. They are flameproof and are made in a range of colours. Cheap enamel pans chip and will burn if used on top of the cooker. All enamel pans are oven to table ware. *Cast iron* is also available in a number of attractive designs which can be taken from oven to table. They are flameproof and as they conduct heat well, they are very efficient to use.

Glass casseroles are easy to use and keep clean. They are inexpensive, too. However, they are only ovenproof, that is, they can't be used on top of the cooker, except for one type made from a special ceramic. *Earthenware*, traditionally used for many casseroles, is also only ovenproof. Reasonable in price, they can be found in many shapes, sizes and colours. *China* casseroles can be expensive but look most attractive on the table. Some are flameproof, otherwise used in the oven only.

Pressure cookers

These cookers cut cooking time and so save money on fuel costs. They are not cheap to buy but if used regularly, they can be a money-saver.

Tins for baking

These can be made of tin or aluminium, with or without non-stick surfaces. A good selection should include two 18 cm/7 inch *sandwich tins* to take a 3-egg mixture, a *Swiss roll tin*, 1 or 2 trays of *bun tins* and, if you like individual Yorkshire puddings, then a tin for them as well. An 18 cm/7 inch *flan ring* can be used for all flans but you can also have fluted ones for making sweet flans. For bread, cakes and pâtés, buy a 450 g/1 lb or 1 kg/2 lb *loaf tin* and an 18 cm/7 inch *cake tin*. You may also like to have a French style sponge tin called a *moule à manqué*, which has sloping sides and is ideal for gâteaux. You will need some fluted and plain *pastry cutters* and a *wire tray* for cooling cakes. A small round one is useful as well as a large oblong tray. You will need 1 or 2 *baking sheets* and *roasting tins*; a second roasting tin can double as a cake tin for making slab cakes.

Boards

Buy a good sized *pastry board*; a marble slab makes an ideal working surface for pastry because it is always cool. You can often buy off-cuts from the stonemason. A smaller sturdy *chopping board* is necessary for everything that needs cutting and chopping, and you may like a *bread board* as well. Boards can be made from wood or plastic laminates, they are easy to take to the sink to clean and will protect your work surfaces from cuts and scratches.

Rolling pins

Choose one which measures slightly more than the width of your pastry board, to enable you to roll out the pastry the full width if necessary. Most rolling pins are made from wood. Glass ones can be bought and some can be filled with iced water to keep the pastry cool.

Spoons and spatulas

A selection of wooden ones is useful. It is a good idea to keep one shape for savoury and another for sweet flavours. Plastic ones can be used, providing they are heatproof. Metal spatulas are ideal for folding in flour and egg whites, and rubber ones for scraping out bowls. *Large metal spoons* for coating or spooning sauce over food, and a *fish slice* for lifting fish or meat, are invaluable. To go with these, you will need a *long pronged fork*, another with a *safety guard* for carving, some *tongs* for lifting food and a *soup ladle*.

Scales and measures

There are 2 types available, either the *spring balance scales* or the *old fashioned scales* with *weights*. It is also wise to buy a set of *measuring spoons*, they are inexpensive.

Whisks

A small hand held *electric beater* will save you a lot of time or you can use a *rotary* one. *Balloon* whisks are good to use when making sauces and a *tennis racket* type or a *spiral* one can be used for other mixtures and cream.

Bowls

You will need a selection of bowls. Buy at least 1 large one for mixing cakes and pastry, and several smaller ones in assorted sizes. Choose from glass, china, stainless steel and plastic. Plastic ones cannot be put into the oven and are not the best for whisking egg whites.

Baking dishes

Buy 1 or 2 *pie dishes* to suit the size of your family and a larger one for entertaining. *Soufflé dishes* and individual *ramekins* can be used for hot soufflés and cold desserts.

Sieves

These are needed for many jobs. Choose a wire one to sift flour and sugar for cakes and pastries. You may use the same one or a similar one for straining liquids; you may prefer the pointed *chinois* made especially for sauces. Icing sugar should not be put through a metal sieve as the metal could discolour the icing. Keep a nylon or plastic one for this alone. *Wooden-sided sieves* with a nylon mesh are good for making fruit purées but, for the average household, a *vegetable mill* will purée soups, fruit and vegetables in the shortest possible time.

Graters, colanders etc.

Use a fine grater for nutmeg and the zest of citrus fruit. Or use a gadget called a *zester* on the fruit. A coarse grater is needed for cheese and vegetables, or choose a small rotary *mouli grater* which produces finely grated foods. It is easy to use and clean.

At least one *colander* is necessary for draining vegetables, rice and pasta. Make certain it has strong firm handles. Choose a *steamer* with a stepped bottom that will fit snugly on to any size pan. (A colander is no substitute, it has too many holes and the steam escapes, making the kitchen very damp instead of cooking the food.)

Miscellaneous equipment

One *jug* for measuring liquids. They are easier to use if you can see the liquid level through them, so glass or plastic are best.

A lemon squeezer is important. Glass ones are cheap and efficient, some plastic ones have containers underneath to catch the juice.

Egg slicers although not essential can cut an egg neatly into slices or wedges, which are useful for garnishing.

If you like the flavour of garlic and don't want the smell on your board or on your hands, buy a *garlic crusher*. *Cherry* and *olive stoners* are gadgets worth buying if you use them enough.

A canelle knife can be used to make decorative grooves on cucumber, oranges and lemons. *Skewers, can opener and scissors* need no explanation.

Other odds and ends which you will find useful are *pot stands* to protect your working surfaces from heat, *flour and sugar dredgers*, a *pepper mill* and *salt pot*, *piping bags* with large *plastic nozzles*, both plain and star, for piping éclairs, potatoes, cream and meringues, and a *hand mincer*, if you don't have one to fit on your mixer. You may also like to have a *sugar thermometer*, and, if there is not one on your cooker, a *timer*. Don't forget to buy a *corkscrew*, one with cantilevered arms is practical.

ELECTRICAL EQUIPMENT

For any cook who does a lot of cooking, a large mixer or food processor is invaluable.

Large mixers
These not only beat and whisk, they have a wide variety of attachments to liquidize, mince, sieve, shred and slice vegetables, grind coffee, extract juice and many other things as well.

Small mixers and liquidizers
You may find it more economical to buy a small mixer and a separate liquidizer. On the other hand, if you do a great deal of cooking you may find it useful to have a hand mixer for small quantities as well as a larger one.

Food processors
Take the hard work out of chopping and shredding vegetables for soups and salads, making pastries, pâtés, breadcrumbs and mayonnaise. They are quick, efficient and labour saving. Prices vary, they can be rather expensive but if you use your machine enough, it can be well worthwhile.

Coffee percolaters and filter machines
If you make a lot of coffee then either of these is useful. If you don't use much coffee then make it in a saucepan or jug, or you can buy a plastic filter holder quite cheaply. *Coffee grinders* certainly come into the 'Will I use it?' category. They are invaluable if you like freshly ground coffee.

Electric deep fryers
These are thermostatically controlled and, therefore, are a safe way of cooking in deep fat or oil. Some have a filter on the top which absorbs the smell of frying. Small ones, holding only 600 ml/1 pint, are also available. It can be a very useful piece of equipment, depending on how regularly you cook deep fried foods.

Slow cookers

Having the advantage of requiring no more electricity than an average electric light bulb, they are economical to use, and especially valuable if you are out all day. The meal can be prepared and put in the cooker before leaving home, it will be ready on return in the evening. Some have a high speed which cooks a stew in 4 hours and a low speed which takes about 8 hours. Some models have an inner casserole that can be taken to the table. They can also be used for cooking oranges and lemons for marmalade, and for keeping punches warm for Christmas parties.

Heated hot plates

Keeping food hot is one of the dilemmas of the cook. A hot plate or food container can help. Plates and covered casseroles can be put on the hot plate to keep hot, leaving the oven free for vegetables and other dishes. A *heated trolley* or *sideboard unit* has vegetable dishes in the top with space underneath for food and/or plates. Most food keeps well in them, but Brussels sprouts and green vegetables are best cooked just before you serve them, and roasted or fried potatoes should not be kept in covered dishes if they are to remain crisp. Hot plates and heated trolleys ease the serving of food, whether for family meals or for entertaining.

Food

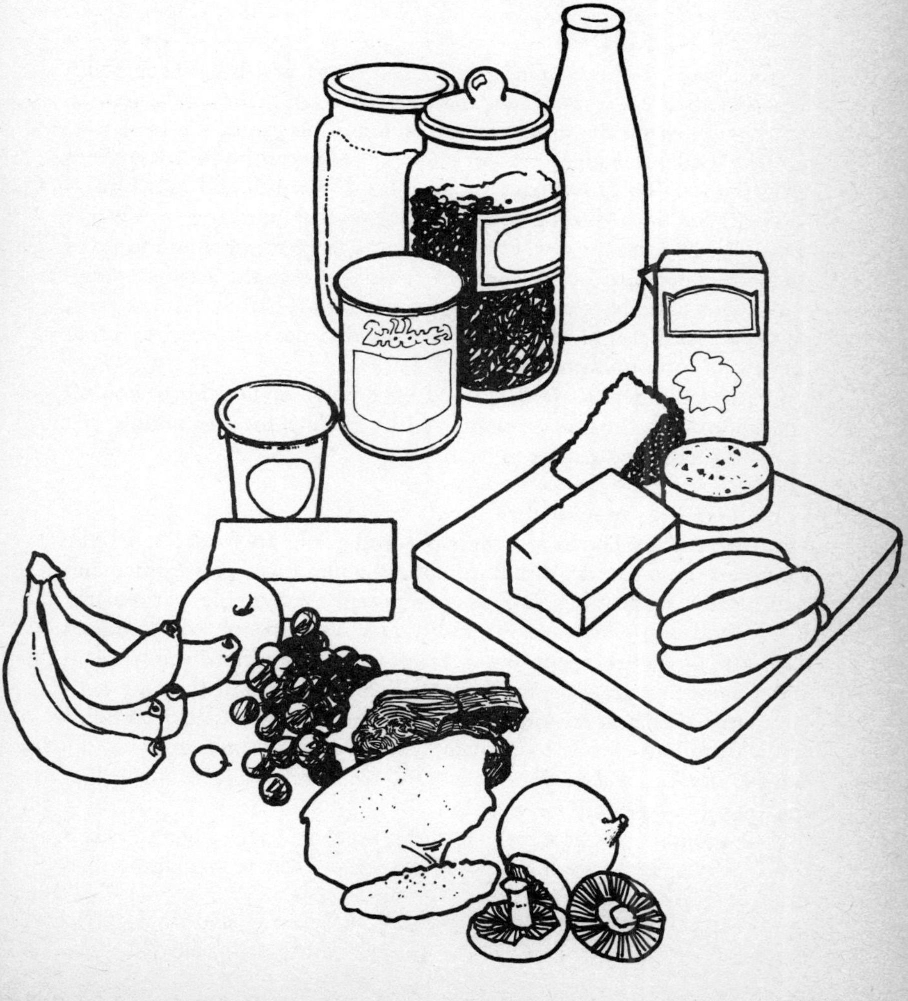

Food safety and hygiene.

In most cases food poisoning results from food which has been badly handled or stored. Carelessness and ignorance can make food unsafe to eat. By following the guidelines given here, this can be avoided.

Most food poisoning germs or bacteria live in our bodies, in animals or in the soil. To grow, bacteria need food, warmth and moisture. If foods are left in the wrong conditions for several hours, e.g. in a warm room, the bacteria are able to multiply to a large number and some of them will produce poisons, called toxins. When the food is eaten, toxins and some bacteria cause food poisoning. Therefore, foods must be stored correctly in the refrigerator, cold larder or freezer to avoid the risk of food poisoning.

Most of the germs are destroyed by boiling or heating to 100°C/212°F. Some toxins can be destroyed by boiling for 30 minutes, but some of them are resistant to heat.

Foods needing special care

Made up dishes The foods where harmful germs are most likely to be found are in made up dishes. Shepherd's pie, meat pies, mince and dishes made with milk and eggs are especially vulnerable, particularly if hot food is allowed to cool slowly in a warm room. Cool cooked food rapidly and then put in the refrigerator. Pasteurized milk, cream and products made with them can become a hazard, if they are contaminated after heat treatment. Keep all cooked and pasteurized foods apart from raw foods to prevent contamination, and store in the refrigerator or cold larder. Take care when reheating food, heat it thoroughly as quickly as possible.

Gravy should not be kept overnight, unless in the refrigerator. It is much safer to make fresh gravy the next day; meat and fish aspic are a particular risk.

Poultry, game and pork These must be completely defrosted and cooked thoroughly. A large number of reported cases of food poisoning are traced to poultry: frequently, poultry carries salmonella food poisoning germs, but if the bird is cooked thoroughly, the germs are killed and there is no danger. If it is not completely defrosted, it may not cook right the way through. The moist warm conditions inside the bird are ideal for the growth of the salmonella and a potential health hazard. When game is hung, it could at the same time encourage the growth of food poisoning germs. These will be killed if it is cooked properly (see cooking times on page 170). Pork can be infected by the cysts or larvae of parasitic worms but providing the meat is completely cooked through, there is no danger to health.

Never partly cook meat or poultry and then finish cooking it later, as this can be extremely dangerous. When food is partly cooked it is only just warmed, providing ideal conditions for the development of food poisoning germs, and the subsequent cooking time may not be long enough to destroy them.

Vinegar, sugar and salt have long been recognized as preservatives because harmful germs cannot grow in them. Therefore, food containing a high concentration of these such as pickles, jams, honey etc., are unlikely to cause food poisoning.

Hygiene in shops

The laws relating to food hygiene in shops are strict and explicit, and environmental health officers are on constant watch to guard your right to buy wholesome food. More food poisoning is caused by carelessness and ignorance than a flagrant disregard to the laws. It is your responsibility to buy from shops with a consistently high standard of cleanliness. If you are dissatisfied with the standard of hygiene in the shop, tell the owner or manager. If you are still not satisfied, change your supplier. You should report any bad instances of lack of hygiene to your local health officer.

Transporting shopping

As germs like warmth, one of the hazards of shopping is keeping food cool. It is so much easier and convenient to buy essential foods first but, on a hot day, never carry meat or other perishable foods for several hours in the bottom of a shopping basket or leave it in a car parked in the hot sun. Plan shopping so that meat, fish and other perishable foods can be taken home and put into the refrigerator as soon as possible. Ensure that fresh meat is well wrapped and make sure that the meat juices do not seep through to other foodstuffs you have bought.

Take care not to put root or salad vegetables on top of perishable foods. Some of the harmful germs live in the soil and if the wrappings get torn, they could contaminate the other food. Carry frozen food in an insulated box or bag, or wrap in plenty of newspaper so that it cannot partially thaw before putting into the freezer.

Hygiene and storage in the kitchen

Make sure all working surfaces and utensils in the kitchen are kept really clean. Raw poultry or meat may leave germs on working surfaces or utensils. Be careful not to contaminate cooked food by placing on the same surface, or using the same utensils unless they have been thoroughly cleaned.

Tea towels and dish cloths must be boiled regularly because they are ideal breeding grounds for harmful bacteria, and an easy way of transferring them from one place to another. Wash the floor regularly and keep the rest of the kitchen clean. All these precautions help, but food is still not safe unless it is stored correctly.

Unwrap all meat and fish, put on a plate and lightly cover with greaseproof paper or cling film. Place immediately on the shelf below the ice-making compartment (which is the coldest shelf) and make sure that the food does not drip on to cooked foods beneath. Keep raw meat and fish and cooked foods apart, so that any germs on the raw meat do not contaminate the cooked food.

Keep salads and vegetables in the crisper drawer in the bottom of the refrigerator. Store root vegetables in the vegetable rack in the larder. Wash lettuce and store in a polythene bag, otherwise the earth on the root or the insects nestling in the leaves could get on to other food. Wash or wipe other vegetables so that there is no earth on them, and always wash fruit and salad vegetables before eating. Put milk into the refrigerator soon after delivery. If this is not possible, make sure the milkman leaves it in a shady place where the birds cannot peck off the tops. Always wipe the outside and bottom of milk bottles before placing in the refrigerator.

Personal hygiene

This can so easily be taken for granted. Always wash your hands before preparing food and particularly after handling raw meat or poultry, after visiting the lavatory or changing a baby's nappy, or after doing dirty jobs like washing the floor. Cuts and sores can be a germ breeding ground, so keep them well covered with waterproof dressings. When you have a bad cold or feel ill, try not to handle food. This is a time when a pre-packed frozen or packet meals could be of use.

Protection from flies, etc.
Flies, domestic animals and vermin can all bring infection into the kitchen. Flies carry harmful germs. The way to avoid contamination from them is to keep the necessary foods in the refrigerator or under a flyproof cover. Eliminate, as far as possible, the places where they breed especially where food can accumulate. Empty and wash frequently all kitchen waste bins. Dustbins with tight fitting lids must be kept clean, and should be placed away from kitchen and larder doors and windows. A fine mesh screen over a larder window will help to keep insects out and will let the cool air in.

Domestic animals can also carry infection, so keep your pets away from family food. Use separate utensils for their food and wash them separately from the family dishes. Never allow pets to jump on the working surfaces.

CORRECT FOOD STORAGE

The larder
With care, perishable foods can be kept in a cool larder. Make certain the larder is well ventilated by a fine mesh covered window or an air brick. One shelf should be made of slate or marble, or tiled because these surfaces always remain cool. Keep all raw and cooked food under a flyproof cover or in a meat safe, but make sure they are kept separate. Don't keep leftover canned meat overnight, use it the same day. In hot weather, milk and butter can be kept cool under special porous earthenware covers, or by covering the bottle or butter dish with a clean wet cloth and standing it in a bowl of cold water. Unless the larder is very cold, it is inadvisable to store cream, cream cakes and custards. Obviously, the time of year and the temperature in the larder will affect the length of time food can be stored.

The storage times given in the chart are the maximum time food can be safely kept in a larder in cold weather. In the summer, it is best to buy and eat perishable foods as you need them.

The refrigerator
The refrigerator is for the storage of perishable food for a short time only, as the growth rate of germs only slows down at this temperature. Commercially packed frozen food can be kept in the ice storage

compartment for short periods, according to the star rating indicated on the door of the compartment. It must not be used for freezing fresh food because it is not equipped to do so.

Make sure all food containers put into the refrigerator are clean. Don't let stale food accumulate in the refrigerator, check it frequently. Cover meat, fish and cooked meats to prevent drying out and put them in the coldest part under the ice compartment. All food must be cool before it is put into the refrigerator. A large volume of warm food will raise the temperature in the cabinet which may spoil other foods, and it will also cause excessive icing. Cover strong smelling foods, such as cheeses and cut melon, so that they don't flavour other foods, particularly milk, butter, cream and bacon.

Defrost the refrigerator every week. If the ice compartment is full of food, take it out, wrap in clean newspaper and defrost the refrigerator quickly by putting bowls of hot water inside and leaving the door open. Wash the inside of the cabinet regularly with a little bicarbonate of soda in hot water. Don't use a detergent as this could leave a smell. Dry the inside of the cabinet thoroughly before replacing the food.

The freezer

Food can be kept safely in the freezer for a long time, as any germs present are dormant until the food is defrosted.

Keep your freezer in a cool dry place with a good circulation of air around it. Wrap all foods in freezer quality bags or containers. Make certain that everything is labelled before being put into the freezer and keep a record of the contents. Don't hoard odds and ends of food unless you know when you are going to use them. Use all foods within its specified storage time. Defrost your freezer about every 6 months or when the ice gets more than 1 cm/½ inch thick. Use bicarbonate of soda in hot water to wash the inside of the freezer, not detergent, and dry.

The refrigerator or freezer should not be kept in the larder. They both need a good intake of air if they are to work properly and, while keeping the inside of the refrigerator or freezer cold, they produce heat which could make your larder too warm for the safe storage of food.

STORAGE TIMES

	In a cold larder	In the refrigerator	In a freezer at – 18°C/0°F
Uncooked meat, poultry and game			
Beef	2 days	3–5 days	1 year
Pork	2 days	2–4 days	6 months
Lamb	2 days	3–5 days	9 months
Veal	2 days	2–4 days	6 months
Bacon rashers	4 days	7 days	1 month
Bacon vacuum packed rashers (unopened)	5 days	7 days	3 months
Mince	Same day	1–2 days	3 months
Offal	1 day	1–2 days	2–3 months
Sausages	1 day	3 days	3 months
Chicken and turkey	1 day	2 days	1 year
Duck and goose	1 day	2 days	4–6 months
Game (after hanging)	Same day	Same day	3–4 months
Cooked meat, poultry and game			
Casseroles with bacon	1 day	2 days	3 months
Casseroles without bacon	1 day	3 days	6 months
Ham	1–2 days	2–3 days	2 months
Meat pies	1 day	1 day	2 months
Sliced meat in gravy	—	2–3 days	3 months
Sliced meat without gravy	1–2 days	2–3 days	2 months
Pâté	1 day	2 days	1 month
Pâté with brandy	2–3 days	1 week	1 month
Poultry and game	1 day	2 days	1–2 months
Fish			
White fish	Same day	2–4 hours	6 months
Smoked fish	1 day	3–4 days	3 months
Shellfish	Same day	24 hours	3 months
Shellfish (defrosted)	As soon as defrosted		Never refreeze

STORAGE TIMES

	In a cold larder	In the refrigerator	In a freezer at – 18°C/0°F
Dairy foods			
Milk	1–2 days	3–4 days	1 month (homogenized)
Cream	Same day	2–3 days	—
Butter, salted (unopened packets)	1–3 weeks	3–4 weeks	3 months
Butter, unsalted (unopened packets)	1–3 weeks	3–4 weeks	6 months
Eggs	1–2 weeks	3 weeks	1 month

The store cupboard

The larder or store cupboard must be cool and dry because cans and packets will deteriorate in the warmth and damp. Wooden shelves are easier to clean if they are covered with stick-on plastic sheeting. The shelves should be within easy reach and shallow ones are best. If they are too deep, food may get pushed to the back and forgotten.

Use airtight containers such as glass or polythene for storing dry groceries and label them clearly. Never put a new supply on top of food already in a container. Finish one quantity, wash and thoroughly dry the container and then refill with new stock. Write the date on cans and packets, so that you use them in the order in which they were bought. Check the stores frequently, if weevils and other insect pests should get into them, throw the food away and wash and dry the storage jars well. Open packets are most likely to attract these insects.

Dented cans of food are often offered at reduced prices, but don't buy them if they are dented or damaged on the seam or rims, or if they are rusty. It is unwise to store damaged cans anyway, as the dents may have cracked the protective coating on the inside. It is safer to use them as soon as possible. Check your store of cans from time to time and if any are blown or leaking, throw them away as they are unsafe to eat. Use all cans and packets within their shelf life.

In the following pages, you will find information about the types of foods which you are likely to keep in your store cupboard.

FATS AND OILS

There are many different fats and oils available. They are important because of the ways they can be used to vary flavours and textures.

Fats provide warmth and energy. Some of them are valuable for the amount of Vitamins A and D they contain, but all are high in calories and have twice as many as protein and carbohydrate foods.

Oils are fats which remain liquid at normal temperatures. They contain the same number of calories as hard cooking fats. The main difference to the cook is that because they are liquid, they can be used in different ways. Oils are not used much in baking, but are an essential ingredient of mayonnaise and salad dressings. Because they contain no water, most oils can be heated to high temperatures without burning, so are excellent for frying.

To the health conscious, particularly those with a history of coronary heart disease, oils are popular because those sold for cooking are vegetable oils and these contain a high proportion of 'polyunsaturated' fats. Polyunsaturated and saturated are descriptions of the chemical structure of the fat. This determines whether a fat remains liquid or hardens. Animal fats contain a large proportion of saturated fats which makes them hard. Most vegetable fats contain a high percentage of polyunsaturated fats which keep them liquid. It is thought that fats of this type can lower the level of cholesterol in the body.

FATS

Margarine Margarine can be bought in hard blocks, or in tubs with a soft spreadable texture, to suit all purposes. One or two margarines are made solely with vegetable oils, but most are made with a mixture of animal and vegetable oils. Vitamins A and D are added during manufacture. This makes margarine an important source of Vitamin D because the supply remains constant the whole year through. Margarine can be eaten in place of butter or used for baking but, because of the water content, it is not suitable for any type of frying.

Margarine spreads or low fat spreads Sold under brand names and, like butter spreads, are made with a high water content and so contain only half the calories of conventional margarine. Generally, Vitamins A and D are added to give the same nutritional value as margarine. Because these spreads contain so much moisture, they are not always suitable for baking or cooking.

White cooking fats Made in a similar way to margarine, but they contain no liquid and can be used for frying as well as baking. They are sold under brand names.

Lard Refined from pig's fat. It should be white in colour with a firm smooth texture, a pleasant smell and a clean taste. Sold ready packaged, lard can be used for pastries, frying and roasting.

Dripping The fat of beef which has been melted down. It has a stronger flavour and firmer texture than lard and is not generally used for baking. Use for frying and roasting.

Suet The fat which surrounds the kidney in beef. It can be bought from the butcher and then finely grated or chopped to use in suet pastry or puddings. It is easier to chop if a little flour is sprinkled on the board; the membranes can easily be removed at this stage. Most suet is commercially shredded and then mixed with flour to keep it free flowing. It is then packaged and sold under a brand name.

OILS

Corn oil Made from the germ of the grains of maize. It is a yellow coloured oil and has a mild flavour, making it ideal for all culinary purposes. Because corn oil can be heated to high temperatures without spoiling, it is particularly useful for deep frying.

Groundnut or arachide oil Made from the groundnut (peanut). It is a pale yellow oil with little or no flavour. Very good for mayonnaise and salad dressings, but because this oil is so bland, it needs plenty of seasoning. Can also be used for shallow and deep frying.

Soya bean oil Extracted from the soya bean. The flavour is a little more definite than some other vegetable oils, but it can be used for all culinary and cooking purposes.

Sunflower oil Pressed from the seeds of the sunflower and, like olive oil, only needs to be filtered. It has a pleasant flavour and is high in polyunsaturates. Excellent for salad dressings.

Blended vegetable oils Made from a mixture of any vegetable oils. The flavour will vary with the types used.

Walnut oil This has a delicate but distinctive flavour of walnuts, and is made in the Perigord and Dordogne regions in France. It is not often sold in this country but is well worth buying if available, as it is excellent for salad dressings. Buy in small quantities as this oil does not keep well.

Olive oil The oldest and possibly the best known of all culinary oils. The oil is obtained by pressing the crushed stoned fruit. All olive growing countries produce oil with special colour and characteristic flavour.

The best French oils come from Provence and have a delightful fragrant taste. Spain and Italy also export very good quality olive oil, both have a lighter flavour than some of the other olive oils on the market.

Good quality olive oil is the least refined of all the oils. It is filtered after pressing, but is not processed in any other way. Olive oil gives an excellent flavour to mayonnaise, salad dressings, many sauté chicken dishes and meat or vegetable stews, especially those from the Mediterranean region such as poulet sauté à la provençale or ratatouille. It should not be used for deep frying because it cannot be heated to a high enough temperature without burning. Olive oil is the most expensive oil to buy and, as it contains only a moderate amount of polyunsaturates, is not suitable to use in cholesterol lowering diets.

Mineral oils Liquid paraffin comes into this category. They are chemically different to food fats and oils, although their appearance is similar. Mineral oils cannot be utilized by the body, but function as laxatives, and will reduce the absorption of some nutrients. Must not be used for cooking.

Fat for deep frying

For successful deep frying, it must be possible to make the fat or oil sufficiently hot to cook the food without the fat or oil burning or spoiling. The temperature at which fats start to smoke or burn is called the 'smoking point', this is much higher in some than others. To give the best flavour to deep fried foods and to cook more safely, choose a fat with a smoking point higher than the temperature needed to cook the food. Deep fried foods are cooked at temperatures between 160–195°C/320–390°F. Electric thermostatically controlled deep fat fryers will give the correct temperature at the touch of a switch. Otherwise, use a thermometer or test the temperature with a small cube of bread: at 160°C/320°F it will become brown in 60 seconds. At 175°C/360°F it takes 40 seconds. At 195°C/390°F, it takes 20 seconds. Fats such as butter and margarine, which contain salt and water, have low smoking points and cannot be used for deep frying.

Smoking points of fats and oils

TYPE OF FAT	Smoking temperature °C	°F
Butter	148	300
Margarine	155	311
Dripping	163	325
Olive oil	169	353
Concentrated butter for cooking	190	374
Lard	190	374
Cooking oil (groundnut)	218	424
Cooking oil (corn)	221	430
Cooking fat	224	435

GELATINES AND JELLIES

There are several types of products on the market for making jellies. Gelatine is the one which is most familiar, and is made by refining animal bones and tissue. There are two types that the housewife can buy, powdered and leaf. They have the same setting power and uses, but vary in their appearance, flavour and the way they are prepared.

Powdered gelatine This is the most readily available. It can be purchased in boxes containing several packets. Each packet or 3 teaspoons of powdered gelatine weighs approximately 15 g/½ oz and will set 600 ml/1 pint.

Leaf gelatine Made in thin transparent sheets and sold in 1 and 2 kg/2 and 4½ lb boxes. Some grocers and delicatessen shops will sell it in smaller quantities. Leaf gelatine is not so readily available as powdered gelatine, but is well worth buying as it has no flavour and dissolves easily. Use 15 g/½ oz to set 600 ml/1 pint.

Fruit jellies These are made from gelatine and fruit juices or fruit flavourings.

Aspic This is a savoury jelly. You can make your own or buy it in granules, powder, in packets or drums. Add boiling water to dissolve it and then it is ready to use.

Agar-agar A vegetable gelatine-like product. It is widely used in commercially prepared foods and can be purchased in sheets. Health food shops are the best places to buy it. Agar-agar has a greater setting power than gelatine and only small quantities need to be used. Because it is a vegetable product, it is popular with vegetarians and people who do not wish to mix milk with animal proteins.

Isinglass The purest form of gelatine and also the most expensive. It is made for the swimming bladder of fish, especially sturgeon.

Carrageen (or Irish) moss Made from a seaweed, which is dried and blanched and can be used as a substitute for gelatine. To use carrageen moss, soak it and then simmer until jelly like. Sieve before using.

FLOUR

Flours are made from grains of wheat which are ground, then graded according to the amount of bran and wheat germ left after milling.

Wholemeal or wholewheat flours These flours are 100 per cent extraction. This means that the whole of the wheat grain has been ground, nothing has been added and nothing taken away.

Wheatmeal or brown flour This contains 85–90 per cent of the wheat grain. Wholemeal and wheatmeal flours can be coarse, medium or fine ground.

Stoneground flour Milled in the traditional way by grinding the cleaned grain between two grooved stones. All parts of the grain are kept in the flour and this is a 100 per cent extraction. It is a coarse flour and makes a delightful nutty bread. Some flour is sieved to remove the larger particles, and this is then sold as an 81 per cent stoneground flour.

White flour During the milling of white flour, most of the bran and wheatgerm, which give colour and flavour to wholemeal and brown flour are removed. It is a 72–74 per cent extraction. Some of the bran and wheatgerm is added to speciality breads, and some is sold under brand names.

Strong or bread flour Some of the proteins in flour, when mixed with water, form gluten. When a dough is kneaded and worked, it becomes pliable and stretches like elastic due to the gluten toughening. This is a great benefit when making bread and some pastries. Strong flours contain a high proportion of these gluten forming proteins.

Weak or soft flour This comes from the soft winter wheat. It contains less of the gluten forming proteins, but more starch.

All purpose flour This is the white flour most housewives buy, and it can be either plain or self-raising. The miller mixes strong and soft flours to give one best suited to everyday cooking; the amounts of each vary with different brands. To test the flour, pick up a handful and squeeze it gently, then open your hand. Strong flour flows freely and soft flour remains clogged together.

Self-raising flour A plain flour which has chemical raising agents added to it. Every 450 g/1 lb self-raising flour contains the equivalent of 4 teaspoons baking powder.

Super sifted flours These are made to give even sized particles that flow easily. This prevents them clogging together, making it less likely for a mixture to go lumpy.

Speciality flours Flours are milled from other cereals as well, such as rye, barley and oats. These tend to be expensive because of their limited production. Rye flour contains only a small proportion of the gluten forming proteins. Barley and oat flours yield no gluten at all. Other flours contain a mixture of various cereals, e.g. granary flour contains malted wheat and rye.

The effect on your cooking

Because of the high proportion of bran and wheatgerm retained in wholemeal and brown flours, bread, cakes and pastries made with them have a closer texture and will rise less than those made with white flour. By using half white and half wholemeal, or brown flour, they will have a more open texture and a lighter colour.

Gluten can be toughened or weakened by the addition of other ingredients. It can be toughened by salt. Too little or no salt in bread gives a sticky dough. As acidity will also tighten a dough, sometimes lemon juice is added to puff or flaky pastry. Use a strong flour for these pastries and there is no need to add lemon juice. Handling, kneading and mixing will also tighten the gluten. This is necessary in bread and other yeast doughs, but not pastry doughs.

The bran and wheatgerm in wholemeal and brown flours will weaken the gluten, therefore bread made with them will have less volume and a closer texture. High levels of fat, egg and sugar will also weaken the gluten. Because of this, brioche, babas and other rich doughs need more yeast or a longer time to rise than bread doughs.

WHICH WHITE FLOUR TO USE

Bread and other yeast doughs. Puff, flaky and choux pastries.	Strong flour.
Rich cakes and puddings such as Victoria sandwiches, castle puddings, suet pastry etc.	Soft all purpose flour, either self-raising or a plain one with baking powder.
Rich fruit cakes, whisked sponges, shortcrust and all other pastries other than those mentioned above.	Soft plain all purpose flour.
Thickening sauces and soups etc.	Any plain flour.
Biscuits and shortbread.	Soft plain all purpose flour.
Yorkshire pudding and pancakes.	Any plain flour. The gluten content is too diluted to have any effect.

RICE

There are at least 7,000 known varieties of rice in the world. Because it is an aquatic plant, the rice fields are flooded with water until the grain is almost ready for harvesting. It takes 300 gallons of water to grow 450 g/1 lb rice. Rice is mainly carbohydrate, containing a little protein and small amounts of the B vitamins, iron and calcium.

Brown rice The whole unpolished long grain of rice with only the husk and a small amount of bran removed. It has a nutty flavour and, because the germ of the grain is retained, it contains larger amounts of vitamins, minerals and protein. It takes longer to cook than white rice, about 40 minutes.

Long grain rice This is still often known as Patna rice. It originated from north east India, but now most supplies come from America. The grains are long and slim, and when cooked will keep light and fluffy. Serve with curries, stews, chicken, meat dishes, or in salads.

Basmati rice This is a fine quality long grain rice from India. It has an excellent flavour and is ideal to serve with curries. Look for it in your local Indian food shop.

Short grain rice Called round or pudding rice, (was known as Carolina rice) and most of it is grown in Italy. Uncooked, short grain rice has a chalky appearance and when cooked is slightly sticky. In this country, it is generally used for puddings or moulds, but is used in many Continental recipes for risottos and other savoury dishes.

Italian or risotto rice This has plump grains slightly larger than short grain rice and is, of course, excellent for risottos.

Arborio rice This comes from northern Italy and is a specific risotto rice with a delicious flavour.

Easy to cook rice This rice has been partly cooked by steam under pressure. It has a more translucent and slightly waxy appearance than ordinary rice. The darker appearance is due to the extra protein which is retained during processing. Because it is cooked before milling, this rice also contains more vitamins and minerals. It has the advantage of producing tender, separate grains. Although it is easy to cook in a measured amount of water, easy to cook rice takes longer than conventional rice to cook.

Pre-cooked or instant rice Long grain rice which is completely cooked and then dehydrated, and only needs to be reconstituted in hot water. It is usually sold under brand names.

Flaked rice The grains have been processed into flakes. Because it cooks quickly, flaked rice is useful for quick milk puddings and can be used to thicken soups and stews.

Ground rice The rice grains are ground and coarse, medium or fine are available. Use for milk puddings. Fine ground rice can be added to shortbread to give it a fine crisp texture.

Rice flour (Crème de riz) Finely milled rice. Use in recipes to give a fine textured cake or shortbread, or to thicken soups and sauces.

Wild rice This is not actually rice at all, but is the seed from a wild grass. It is particularly delicious with game, but expensive and not readily available.

Rice paper In spite of its name, rice paper is not made from rice. This thin edible paper is made from the pith of a tree which grows in China. It is used for macaroons and other mixtures which need a dry edible base.

SUGAR

Sugar is made from both sugar cane and sugar beet. Before it is ready to eat, it is put through many processes, called refining, to extract impurities. Raw cane sugar goes through the least processes and white sugar the most. Raw cane sugar comes entirely from the cane, other sugars come from both cane and beet. They both have the same sweetness, but brown sugars, black treacle and molasses have a stronger flavour and some taste rather bitter.

Sugar is almost pure carbohydrate and the only real function it has is to provide energy. Molasses and black treacle contain reasonable amounts of calcium and iron, but brown sugars contain such small amounts of vitamins and minerals, they make no significant contribution to our dietary needs. They are no better for you than white sugar but because they have a much stronger flavour, perhaps you may consume less.

WHITE SUGARS

Granulated sugar This sugar has medium sized crystals. It is the most popular sugar sold and is the cheapest. Use for tea, coffee, cereals, fruit, custards, sugar syrups and caramels, in fact anything except cakes, pastries, biscuits and sponges. If granulated sugar is used for baking, sometimes the grains caramelize before they have dissolved and show as small brown specks.

Caster sugar This sugar has the finest crystals. It dissolves quickly and is ideal for all baking. Because it is finer, it is best to serve at the table with strawberries and other fruits, and for sprinkling on fruit pies.

Icing sugar Made by grinding sugar crystals to a fine powder. It dissolves easily and is used in most icings and buttercreams. It can also be used in some meringue mixtures to give a fine soft texture.

Cube or lump sugar Originally called loaf sugar because it was made in conical shaped loaves. It is now made from granulated sugar which is moistened, pressed and cut into neat shapes.

Preserving sugar The large crystals in this sugar dissolve slowly and do not settle in a dense layer on the bottom of the pan. Therefore, jams and other preserves need less stirring to prevent them burning. It also produces less scum and, for these reasons, has the advantage over granulated sugar; it is more expensive, however. Preserves made with granulated sugar will set just as well and have the same clarity.

Coffee sugar Specially made in large crystals and dissolves slowly. It was originally made this way for people who liked the first few sips of coffee to be bitter, then sweetening towards the bottom of the cup. Coffee sugar can be white or coloured, but they all have exactly the same sweetness.

BROWN SUGARS

These can be made from raw cane sugar, or manufactured from either white sugar or cane sugar which has been washed to give it a lighter colour. They are then coloured and flavoured with molasses, and are called 'manufactured sugars'. The labels on the sugar packets tell you exactly what you are buying. If it is raw cane sugar, it states this on the label and also names the country of origin. Manufactured sugar usually has an ingredients list stating 'sugar and molasses' or 'cane sugar and molasses', but there is no country of origin on the label.

Raw cane sugar Called Barbados, Muscovado or Molasses sugar. They are dark brown with small soft sticky grains which clog together. These sugars give excellent colour and flavour to rich fruit cakes and gingerbreads. Raw cane sugar can also be bought in cubes. It is produced in the same way as white cube sugar.

Soft brown sugar These are manufactured sugars and described as light, golden, dark or rich according to the colour. They contain less moisture than raw cane sugar and have a milder flavour.

Demerara sugar This sugar has large golden yellow crystals and, up until 1971, was all made in Guyana. These days, supplies from there are limited, so demerara sugar is now also manufactured from either white sugar or washed cane sugar which is coloured and flavoured with molasses.

MOLASSES, TREACLE AND SYRUPS

Molasses This is the residue left after the sugar has been crystallized from the raw cane or beet juice. Only cane molasses is sold in the shops. Cane molasses has a strong bitter taste and is not as sweet as sugar.

Black treacle Also comes from the residue liquid. It is thinner than molasses and not quite so bitter. Use in making treacle toffee, gingerbread and rich fruit cakes.

Golden syrup Made from the liquid left after the white sugar has been crystallized. Use it for flapjacks, brandy snaps and for sweetening stewed fruit as well as treacle tarts and puddings.

Dark syrup Similar to golden syrup but a little darker with a slightly stronger flavour. Use as for golden syrup. It makes delicious toffee and barbecue sauce.

Maple syrup This is not made from cane or beet, but comes from the sap of the maple tree. It is popular in North America but expensive to buy in this country.

TEXTURED VEGETABLE PROTEIN - TVP

For most people, the word protein means mainly meat but dried peas and beans, nuts and cereals are also protein foods. In fact, a third of the protein in the average UK diet comes from plants. For centuries, soya has been eaten in China as a vegetable. Soya beans and soya flour have been available for many years in this country, but it is only in the last decade or so that food technologists have been able to make use of its full potential. They are now able to produce the proteins from soya, and other peas and beans, in a form resembling the texture of meat. This makes these proteins more acceptable to the average housewife and, of course, is a cheaper and more efficient way of producing protein than obtaining it from meat.

This product is called TVP – Textured Vegetable Protein. You can buy it in packs as flakes and granules, in cans in the form of mince or chunks, either as a ready-to-heat meal, or to mix with meat or mince in casseroles and stews.

It is important to remember that TVP is not a synthetic food, but is a modern adaption of well known and accepted foods. When fortified with iron and some B vitamins, it can be used in place of meat.

TVP is an excellent food for vegetarians and can be used as an economy food to extend the quantity of meat you buy. For the best results, use 25 per cent TVP to 75 per cent meat. About 25 g/1 oz TVP is equal to 100 g/4 oz fresh mince. It is often added to manufactured meat pies and beefburgers to lower the cost, but the labels on these foods must state that TVP has been included in the ingredients.

VINEGAR

Each different kind of vinegar has its own special uses.

Wine vinegar As the name implies, this vinegar is made from either red or white wine. It has a finer flavour than other vinegars and should be used at the table, and in all salad dressings and mayonnaise. Red and white wine vinegars are interchangeable.

Cider vinegar Made from apples, this vinegar is a pale yellow, the colour of apple juice. It has a good flavour, use as wine vinegar.

Malt vinegar This is made from malted barley. It is brown in colour and, because of the strong flavour, is best for chutneys and pickles, sousing fish etc. Malt vinegar is much cheaper than wine vinegar.

Pickling or spiced vinegar This is malt vinegar which has been flavoured with pickling spices and is ready to use for pickling onions, red cabbage etc.

Distilled vinegar A colourless vinegar with a sharp flavour, distilled from malt vinegar. Use for white pickles, such as silverskin onions, and for making cooked salad dressings.

Flavoured vinegars Wine vinegar flavoured with tarragon, mint, chillies, garlic or other herbs and spices can be bought. However, it is easy and cheaper to make your own.

Non brewed condiment This is made from acetic acid and coloured with caramel to make it look like malt vinegar. It is the cheapest you can buy and has a sharp flavour.

YEAST

There are two ways to buy yeast for home baking.

Fresh yeast This is called compressed or distiller's yeast and can be bought in small quantities from some bakers who make their own bread or from health food shops. It should have a moist firm texture, a creamy fawn colour and a clean smell. Stale yeast will look dry, may have an unpleasant odour and should not be used. Fresh yeast will keep in a polythene bag or container in the refrigerator for 2 weeks. It can be frozen for up to 6 weeks. To pack for the freezer, cut into the weights needed for each baking. Place each piece into a small polythene bag or wrap in cling film. Put all the pieces together in one large polythene bag. When needed, blend the yeast into the warm liquid as soon as it is removed from the freezer, as frozen yeast will start to cream if it is left too long.

Dried yeast This yeast can be bought in drums or packets. If you don't make bread often, packets will probably be more useful as yeast stores well in sealed containers, but will only last 3–4 months when opened. When using dried yeast, you only need half the amount you would use with fresh yeast. To use, mix the dried yeast with the warm liquid and a little sugar. Leave in a warm place until the yeast has dissolved. It should get really frothy in 10 minutes, although if you are using milk it may take a little longer.

If the yeast does not froth, this probably means that it is stale and should not be used.

Storage times

These are dependent upon the right conditions. Packets and cans must be kept cool and dry. Jars of herbs, spices and rennet should be kept in the dark. Opened packets must be closed, and if there is an inner lining, make sure it is tightly folded. Replace the lids of all jars and bottles, and keep well sealed.

Acid fruits, fruit juices, tomatoes and tomato juice must never be left in cans once they are opened. Turn them out into another container and keep covered. It is also better to put other foods into covered containers. They should all be stored in a refrigerator or very cool larder.

FOOD	UNOPENED	OPENED Perishable foods – times from opening. Packets and bottles – times from date of purchase
Biscuits	2 weeks (from sell by date)	2 weeks (from sell by date)
Anchovy essence	1 year plus	1 year plus
Baked beans	2 years	Use within 48 hours
Baking powder	Up to 1 year	Use within 3 months
Cake mixes	1 year	—
Cereals		
Breakfast	1 year	As soon as possible
Oatmeal	1 month	1 month
Rice, sago, tapioca	1 year	1 year
Cocoa and drinking chocolate	Up to 1 year	Up to 1 year
Coffee		
Ground fresh	—	Use within 7 days
Ground vacuum packed	Up to 2 years	Use within 7 days
Instant	Indefinitely	As soon as possible
Cornflour	3 years plus	3 years plus
Custard		
Powder	2–3 years	2–3 years
Instant	1 year	1 year
Crisps	1 week	Use immediately
Fish		
Canned in oil	5 years	Use within 24 hours
Canned in sauce	2 years	Use within 24 hours
Pastes	Up to 1 year	Use within 24 hours
Flavouring essences	1–2 years	1–2 years
Food colourings	Indefinitely	Indefinitely
Fruits, canned		
Blackberries	18 months	1–2 days
Gooseberries	18 months	1–2 days
Blackcurrants	18 months	1–2 days

FOOD	UNOPENED	OPENED Perishable foods – times from opening. Packets and bottles – times from date of purchase.
Fruits, canned cont.		
Strawberries	18 months	1–2 days
Raspberries	18 months	1–2 days
Plums	18 months	1–2 days
Prunes	1 year	1–2 days
Rhubarb	1 year	1–2 days
Other fruits	2 years	1–2 days
Fruits, dried	12–15 months	12–15 months
Fruit drinks		
Bottles (squash)	1 year	Use within 3 months
Bottles, juices	1 year	Use within 48 hours
Bottles, ready to drink	1 year	Use within 48 hours
Packets, powder	1 year	Reconstituted, use within 48 hours
Gelatine		
Leaf	Indefinitely if kept dry	Indefinitely if kept dry
Powdered	Indefinitely if kept dry	Indefinitely if kept dry
Herbs	6 months	6 months (freeze dried herbs will keep a better flavour than air dried).
Margarine	4 months	4 months
Mayonnaise, bottled	6 months	2 months in the refrigerator
Meat		
Canned stews, mince etc.	2 years	Use within 24 hours
Canned cold meats such as luncheon meat, ham, corned beef	5 years	Use within 2 days
Ham		
Pasteurized only	9 months – must be kept in the refrigerator. (Bought from the chilled cabinet not from the shelf.)	Use within 48 hours

FOOD	UNOPENED	OPENED Perishable foods – times from opening. Packets and bottles – times from date of purchase.
Paste	Up to 1 year	Use within 24 hours
Milk		
Canned evaporated	3 months	Use as fresh milk
Condensed	1 year	Use as fresh milk
Dried (except for baby milk)	6 months	6 months – use as fresh milk when reconstituted
Baby milk	3 months	3 weeks – use within 24 hours when reconstituted
Puddings	1 year	Use the same day
Nuts	3 months	3 months
Oils		
Cooking and salad	10–18 months	10–18 months
Pasta		
Canned	2 years	Use within 48 hours
Dried	Indefinitely	Indefinitely
Pickles	1 year	1 year
Rennet	Reasonable time	6 months
Salad cream	1 year	2–3 months
Salad dressings		
Coleslaw type	6 months	6 months
Oil and vinegar	9 months	9 months
Sauces		
Horseradish, tartare etc.	6 months	6 months
Tomato, brown etc.	1 year	1 year
Soups		
Canned	2 years	Use within 24 hours
Packets	1 year	Use within 24 hours when reconstituted
Spices		
Peppercorns	Indefinitely	Indefinitely
Other whole spices	1 year	1 year
Ground pepper, curry powder, mustard	1 year	1 year
Others	6 months	6 months

FOOD	UNOPENED	OPENED Perishable foods – times from opening. Packets and bottles – times from date of purchase.
Sugar		
White, brown, icing	Indefinitely	Indefinitely
Stock cubes	1 year	1 year
Syrup	Indefinitely	Indefinitely
Tea	4 months	As soon as possible
Tomatoes		
Canned	Up to 1 year	Use within 48 hours
Juice	Up to 1 year	Use within 48 hours
Purée (tube)	1 year	6 weeks
Purée (jar)	6 months	Use within 48 hours
Purée (can)	Up to 1 year	Use within 48 hours
Vegetables, canned		
New potatoes	18 months	Use within 48 hours
Other vegetables	2 years	Use within 48 hours
Vegetables, dried	1 year	1 year
Vinegar	Indefinitely – keep tightly stoppered	Indefinitely – keep tightly stoppered
Yeast		
Dried	6 months	3–4 months – if tightly sealed and dry
Fresh	—	1–2 weeks in the refrigerator

Dairy produce.

Cheese

Cheese is a versatile food, and it is also very nutritious. All cheeses are an excellent source of protein and calcium, and contain valuable amounts of Vitamins A and D and a little Vitamin B. Weight for weight, most cheese contains about as much protein and 2 to 3 times as much fat as lean meat. About 50–75 g/2–3 oz cheese is as much as most people can eat because of the high fat content, but this supplies nearly all the daily need for protein. Hard cheeses such as Cheddar and Double Gloucester, containing less moisture, have a higher nutritive value than soft ones, such as Camembert and Brie.

Cheesemaking has always been a way of using surplus milk to make a concentrated and easily stored food. Most cheeses take their name from the locality where they were made. Some are still made in their own regions. Roquefort, especially, can only be called by that name if it has been stored within a certain area. For centuries, cheese was made on farms but, with modern technology, it is possible to reproduce the cultures which give cheese its traditional flavour. Most of the cheese we eat today is commercially produced, sometimes a long way from its place of origin.

ENGLISH CHEESE

Cheddar The most popular and easily available of all English cheeses, it is mainly factory produced. Some Farmhouse Cheddar is still made. The colour varies from pale yellow to orange and the flavour from mild to mature. Farmhouse Cheddar is usually sharper and stronger. Cheddar is an excellent cheese for eating, it melts easily and is popular for cooking. Avoid buying if dry, cracked and greasy. It is also imported from New Zealand, Canada, Ireland, Australia and France.

Ilchester Made from Cheddar cheese and flavoured with beer, chives and garlic. It has no rind. Both this and Red Windsor are fairly new additions to the cheese board.

Red Windsor A yellow cheese marbled with red. Made from Cheddar and has no rind. Flavoured with red wine, it tastes slightly sweet.

Caerphilly The youngest of the traditional English cheeses, first made about 150 years ago. A mild tasting white cheese with a close crumbly texture and a slightly sour flavour, reminiscent of buttermilk. Good to eat with salads and celery. Buy Caerphilly as you need it as it does not store well. Moist or yellow looking cheese should not be bought.

Cheshire This is possibly the oldest of our cheeses, being a great favourite of the Romans. Red, white and blue varieties are available. Red Cheshire is an orange colour with a mild nutty flavour and keeps well. White Cheshire is creamy white with the same flavour. It should be eaten fresh as it turns bitter and acid when stale. The texture of both is loose and crumbly. Do not buy either with a greasy or moist surface. Good for cooking or try eating with fruit or fruitcake. Blue Cheshire has a soft buttery texture and a superb flavour. Unfortunately, little is made and it is rather expensive.

Double Gloucester A creamy yellow cheese with a full mellow flavour. It keeps well and is excellent for eating.

Cotswold A recent addition to the cheese board. It is a rindless cheese made from Double Gloucester with chives added.

Derby and Sage Derby Derby is a white cheese with a clean and tangy flavour, which goes well with grapes, pears and apples. Originally Sage Derby was made with an outer coating of sage. The flavour was appealing and the cheese has become popular, particularly around Christmas time. It is now made with the sage mixed into it, to give a green marbled effect. Sage Lancashire and Sage Cheshire are also made.

Wensleydale A white, moderately close, crumbly cheese tasting of buttermilk. Similar to Caerphilly. Ideal for eating with apples and apple pie in the Yorkshire tradition. Do not buy more than you need because it does not store well. A little blue veined Wensleydale is made. It spreads like butter, has a mild creamy flavour and a grey-white rind.

Lancashire A white, soft, crumbly cheese, mild when young. The flavour develops as it matures. It has a more distinctive flavour than Wensleydale and Caerphilly, and is an excellent cheese for cooking as it melts easily.

Leicester Deep orange with a firm texture and mild flavour. An excellent cooking cheese, especially for a traditional Welsh rarebit made with beer.

Stilton White Stilton has a crumbly texture and a slightly sour but mild taste. Blue Stilton, with its mellow creamy flavour, is regarded as the king of English cheeses. It should have a well wrinkled brown rind, pale colour, slightly flaky texture and evenly distributed blue veins. A brown shading near the rind is a sign that the cheese is ripe. White chalky cheeses are too young. It will keep well but if you want a whole one to last for several weeks, buy it slightly immature. It is available all the year and is best from November to April. A whole Stilton weighs about 6.5 kg/14 lb but it is possible, particularly around Christmas time, to buy half a cheese or a smaller 2.25 kg/5 lb one. The way to cut a whole Stilton is to slice it horizontally from the top and then cut into wedges. Scooping it out with a spoon is a wasteful method. Keep the surface covered with foil or cling film to prevent any drying out. Store Stilton at the bottom of the refrigerator or in a cool larder.

Cottage cheese Made from skimmed milk with a cultured cream dressing. Low in calories, it contains about half the protein and an eighth of the amount of fat found in other cheeses. Sometimes flavoured with pineapple, chives etc. Keep in a refrigerator for a few days only. Be aware of the 'sell by' date.

Cream cheese A full fat soft cheese. Made with cream, it has double the fat content of other cheeses and only little protein. Keeps for a few days only in the refrigerator.

Curd cheese A non-specific term referring to soft cheeses e.g. ricotta or low fat soft cheese. Will keep for 2–3 days in the refrigerator.

Lactic cheese A low fat soft cheese which has been soured by special cultures to give the required acidity. The curd is drained and processed before packing in foil.

SCOTTISH CHEESE

Dunlop This is a cheese very similar to Cheddar but is moister in texture and lighter in colour. It is usually eaten quite young and goes well with oatcakes and Scottish ale.

Orkney Another typical Scottish cheese, very similar in texture and flavour to Dunlop. The colour can be white or deep orange. Some cheese from Orkney is smoked.

Scotland is the home of some delightful tasting cream or soft cheeses. **Caboc** is a relatively new one. It is covered in oatmeal and has a slightly sour nutty flavour. **Caithness**, **Islay** from the Hebridean Islands, **Crowdie** and **Howgate** are soft cheeses; they are all well worth looking out for.

FRENCH CHEESE

Camembert Traditionally, it comes from Normandy but is now made in other parts of France and other countries as well. Made into a small disc about 10 cm/4 inch across, it is creamy in colour with a soft white rind and is mostly sold wrapped and boxed. Half cheeses and individual portions can also be bought. Mild and firm when young, as it matures it becomes stronger in flavour but softer in texture. When buying, test by pressing, it should be springy in the centre and softer under the rind. A hard edge, shrinkage in the box and a strong smell of ammonia show that it is stale. Eat Camembert as you like it – fresh, mild and firm, or mature, strong and runny. Most people prefer it when slightly runny with a firm smooth layer in the centre. Eat the rind if you enjoy it. If the cheese is not as ripe as you would like, keep at room temperature until soft. When it's just right, store in the bottom of the refrigerator. Take out about an hour before needed and leave at room temperature to let the flavour develop.

Brie A soft cream cheese similar in texture to Camembert but with a milder flavour. Made into a thin disc shape, a whole Brie measures about 35 cm/14 inch across and weighs about 2.25 kg/5 lb. It is sold in freshly cut portions or pre-packed in wedge shaped boxes. A smaller half size Brie can also be bought. Test and choose in the same way as Camembert. Ripen at room temperature and store, wrapped, in the bottom of the refrigerator.

Munster Comes from the Vosges, and is a round cheese with a deep orange ring and a soft consistency. It smells strong and when it ripens, it tastes strong as well. It is made in small cheeses slightly larger than a Camembert to large ones weighing 1.5 kg/3 lb.

Neufchâtel This is a small creamy cheese and comes from a town near Dieppe. It is best known in a cylinder shape weighing about 100 g/4 oz but is made in square, rectangular and heart shapes as well. It has a soft white rind with a white crumbly texture which becomes creamy as the cheese matures. It has a clean, fresh taste.

Chèvres These are the goat's milk cheeses, made in small or large quantities all over France. One of the best known is Valençay from the Loire which is made in the easily identified pyramid with a flattened top. Chèvre can have a soft white rind or be rindless; sometimes the outside is coated with powdered charcoal or fine sand. Others, such as the Poivre d'Ane, are sprinkled with herbs on the outside. All these cheeses are white with a crumbly texture and a clean, sharp taste.

Carré de l'Est From the Vosges is a small, square, creamy cheese weighing about 100–200 g/4–7 oz. It has a soft white rind with a texture softer than Camembert and a more delicate flavour.

Pont l'Evêque From Normandy, is another square cheese weighing 220 and 400 g/8 and 14 oz. It is a yellow cheese with a pale orange rind. It has a more dominant flavour than Carré de l'Est but smells stronger than it tastes.

Port Salut and St Paulin Port Salut is still made by Trappist monks at their abbey in Port Salut, Normandy. St Paulin is the same type of cheese but made commercially. Pale yellow in colour with a bright orange rind, a mild flavour and smooth resilient texture. It is a round flat cheese weighing about 2.25 kg/5 lb and sold cut into thick wedges, often pre-wrapped. Smaller versions in red and yellow wax are called Baby-Bel and Bonbel. There is a subtle difference in their flavour.

Tomme aux Raisins This is a variety of processed cheese with a black grape pip crust, which gives it a special flavour. It is round, flat and ivory coloured, with a deliciously smooth texture. Sold cut into wedges, sometimes pre-wrapped. Another similar cheese is coated with walnuts which gives it a nutty taste.

Roquefort This has the reputation for being the finest, and the most expensive blue cheese in the world. It is made from ewe's milk and comes from a small area south of the Massif Central. The cheese is stored and ripened in the caves at Combalou and it is there that it acquires the greenish veins and special flavour. The name Roquefort can only be used for cheese ripened in these caves.

It has a soft butter-like texture and a tangy flavour. Good quality cheese should have a brown rind, white inside and an even distribution of veins. Some brown around the inside of the rind is acceptable but avoid crumbling edges or a cheese which is too white with little vein. A whole Roquefort weighs just under 2.75 kg/6 lb and is sold by weight or in pre-wrapped slices.

Bleu de Bresse Small creamy blue cheeses in three sizes – 5, 7.5 or 10 cm/2, 3 or 4 inches across. A cheese in best condition will have a blue-grey mould and when pressed should feel springy but not soft. It will have a slight musty smell but do not buy any which smell too strongly.

Herb cheese Fresh soft cheese blended with herbs and garlic and packed in individual or family size foil packs or plastic tubs. Eat at any time, especially delicious as a filling for baked potatoes. Keep in their original wrapping and store in a polythene container in the refrigerator. They do not store well, so use as soon as possible. Similar cheeses coated with ground or crushed peppercorns are also made.

Petit Suisse A soft, rich cream cheese packed in small plastic or paper containers. The taste is fresh and slightly sour. Served as a dessert with fruit or sugar. Always eaten fresh.

Demi-Sel Similar to Petit Suisse but lightly salted. Packed in foil in small squares.

SWISS CHEESE

Emmenthal Originally it came from the Emme Valley near Berne and is probably one of the most imitated cheeses in the world. The manufacturing process encourages the fermentation which gives Emmenthal its characteristic holes. It has a thick yellow rind and is pale yellow in colour, with a slightly rubbery texture and a mild but distinctive flavour. The holes should be large and even in size and small drops of moisture in them are a sign of good quality. A whole cheese, known as a wheel, weighs about 100 kg/220 lb. Buy freshly cut or pre-wrapped slices. Keeps well and is excellent for eating and cooking e.g. fondues.

Gruyère It has been made in the Fribourg Canton for 700 years, now made in other parts of Switzerland as well. Made in the same way as Emmenthal and somewhat similar in flavour and texture, but is a little sweeter. Pale cream with a slightly oily light brown rind, it has fewer holes than Emmenthal and none should be larger than a pea. Small cracks are a sign of quality. Gruyère wheels weigh about 35 kg/77 lb so buy freshly cut or pre-wrapped slices. Keeps well and is excellent for eating and cooking, especially fondues.

DUTCH CHEESE

Gouda A firm yellow cheese with a mild flavour. Mature Gouda has a fuller salty flavour. Usually made in a flat wheel with a yellow waxed rind weighing about 3–5 kg/7–11 lb. Occasionally sold as Baby Gouda, 300 g/11 oz, with a red waxed rind. Identify Gouda by the official stamp. Gouda has 48 per cent butterfat. It keeps well, is very good to eat and as it melts easily, is excellent for cooking, too.

Edam Easily identified by the round ball shape in red wax, weighing about 2 kg/4½ lb. It is also made in a loaf shape coated with red wax weighing about 3–5 kg/7–11 lb. Look also for the 40 per cent butterfat stamp. It has a mild flavour, is excellent to eat, keeps well and contains less calories than other hard cheeses. A baby Edam weighing about 1 kg/2 lb is also sold.

ITALIAN CHEESE

Gorgonzola It is known to have been made for at least 1,000 years. The colour varies from white to straw colour with blue-green veins and a reddish brown rind. Usually foil wrapped. It has a soft texture and although most Gorgonzola sold in this country has a sharp savoury flavour, it can be much milder and creamy. When over ripe, it turns brown. It can be eaten or used in cooking. Mix with salad dressings or fill pears with it as the Italians do.

Dolcelatte This is the trade name for a creamy Gorgonzola made with pasteurized milk. Smells stronger than it tastes.

Bel Paese Pale yellow cheese with a soft smooth texture and mild flavour. Coated with yellow wax or foil and printed with the greeny-blue trade mark showing the leg of Italy. Individual foil wrapped portions have a creamy texture.

Ricotta This is made from the whey; the by-product after the milk curds have been pressed. Can be made from either ewe's or cow's milk. It has a fresh white crumbly texture with no rind. The flavour is mild with just a hint of sweetness. Often used in lasagne, gnocchi or Italian puddings and cakes.

Mozzarella Originally made from buffalo's milk but most of it is now made from cow's milk. It is a rindless cheese, white in colour with a mild creamy flavour but a strong sour smell and a rubbery texture. It can be eaten when fresh but is mainly used for cooking, especially on pizzas. It is now made in many other countries including Denmark, Canada, Brazil and Argentina.

Parmesan A hard brittle cheese without any holes. Straw yellow in colour with a very distinctive flavour which gets stronger as the cheese ages. Keeps well but can go rancid if not kept cool. Parmesan is made from April to November and is stored for at least 2–3 years or as long as 7–10 years before it is sold. About a year after it is made, Parmesan is sometimes given a protective coating of oil mixed with fine dark earth. The quality of the cheese is tested by striking it with a small hammer and judging the tone of the ring.

It is eaten in Italy as a table cheese when it is young. Mature Parmesan is grated and sprinkled on soups and pasta, and is the type normally sold in this country.

DANISH CHEESE

Samsoe Made in the same way, and originally similar to Emmenthal, but now has its own characteristic flavour from the Danish milk. Pale yellow in colour with holes the size of cherries and a mild nutty flavour that strengthens as the cheese ages. It is made in a large wheel and weighs about 14 kg/31 lb. Samsoe keeps well, is good to eat and can be used grated or thinly sliced for cooking.

Danbo A square cheese similar in colour to Samsoe but with a softer texture. Often flavoured with caraway seeds.

Havarti Made in a block or flat disc and covered with gold foil. It has a firm texture with many small holes. Flavour is slightly sour and sharp, and it has a distinctive smell. Keeps well.

Danish Blue, Danablu A firm, white, crumbly cheese with dark blue-green veins and very sharp salt flavour. Keeps well.

Mycella Another blue cheese from Denmark. It has less veining than Danablu, with a creamier texture and a piquant flavour. It is easy to spread or slice.

NORWEGIAN CHEESE

Jarlsburg A pale yellow cheese with large holes and a yellow rind. It has a slightly rubbery texture and a mild nutty flavour with a hint of sweetness. Good for eating. Melts easily so is useful for cooking and is a good alternative to Gruyère. Keeps well.

Gjetost A brown fudge like cheese made from goat's milk.

STORING CHEESE

Cheese must be protected from air, light and heat. It is best stored in the door or bottom shelf of the refrigerator. Wrap in foil or cling film and keep in a polythene container. Soft cheese, such as Camembert, should be stored cut side up so that the cheese does not run out of the rind. In a cold larder, cheese can be kept under a cheese cover, providing it has been wrapped first.

In warm conditions it is most important to store cheese correctly as hard cheese oils and becomes mouldy. A slight mould can be cut away from the cheese and the rest is edible, but the flavour will usually be spoiled.

Uncovered cheese becomes hard but it can be grated and used for cooking. Soft cheese will ripen quickly if kept in the warm and if it is not wrapped, will form an unappetizing skin. Cream, soft and cottage cheese deteriorate quickly unless stored in the cool. Check the date stamp when you buy these cheeses and eat them as soon as you can. If a rancid smell develops, throw the cheese away, as it is unfit to eat.

To get the best flavour from your cheese, take it from the refrigerator or cold larder and leave at room temperature for about an hour before it is to be eaten.

FREEZING CHEESE

Hard and semi-hard cheese can be frozen. The texture of hard cheese will change and it will tend to crumble when defrosted. It will not be so good for eating, but it is quite satisfactory for cooking. Choose your cheese in the best condition and cut into portions that can be used within 7 days for hard cheese and 3 days for softer ones. Hard cheese will keep for 6–9 months without deterioration of flavour, semi-hard will keep for 4 months and grated cheese for 3 months. Soft cheeses, like Brie and Camembert, do not freeze well. They can develop a strong ammonia flavour if kept for longer than 4–5 weeks. If you want to freeze them, make certain they are firm. Do not freeze ripe cheeses because they continue to mature slowly. Cheese is much better to eat if you let it thaw slowly and thoroughly first. Grated cheese can be used straight from the freezer for cooking.

Milk

Cow's milk is the most complete of all the foods we consume. 600 ml/1 pint supplies half the calcium needed each day by pregnant and nursing women and sufficient for everyone else. It is also a good source of high quality protein, Vitamin A and riboflavin (one of the B vitamins). The small amount of iron and Vitamins C and D are insufficient for a balanced diet.

Milk is a perishable food which deteriorates quickly if it is not stored properly, so the following care should be taken.

- ☐ Take milk indoors as soon as it is delivered or make certain it is left in the cool and in the shade out of direct light. Sunlight destroys Vitamin C and riboflavin.
- ☐ Store in the refrigerator or on a cold shelf in a cool larder.
- ☐ Make certain it is kept in a clean container. The delivery bottle or carton is best, as it was sterilized before being filled with milk. Also, unopened bottles or cartons are not likely to pick up unwelcome flavours from other foods in the refrigerator.
- ☐ Milk jugs should be covered when out of the refrigerator to protect them from dust and flies.
- ☐ Never refill a jug. Rinse used milk jugs in cold water first, then wash them. For extra safety, scald in boiling water and allow to drain.
- ☐ Use milk in rotation.

BUYING AND STORING MILK

All milk sold in the United Kingdom comes from tubercular tested (TT) cows and is heat treated to improve its quality, except for a little sold from specially licensed farms. It is graded according to the heat treatment used.

It is not always realized that when milk has been pasteurized it will not become soured, if kept for too long it will go bad instead.

Fresh cream cheese cannot be made in the home from pasteurized milk. This can only be made with untreated milk. Commercially manufactured cream cheese is made by adding special cultures to the pasteurized milk in a similar way to yogurt.

MILK IN ENGLAND AND WALES

Pasteurized (Silver foil top)
The milk is heated for a few seconds only and cooled rapidly. The temperature is high enough to kill any disease carrying organisms and most of the bacteria which sour milk, but it is not high enough to alter the flavour. The creamline shows at the top of the bottle. This is the milk most generally used for drinking and cooking.
Storage time: 1–2 days in a cool larder. 2–3 days in a refrigerator.

Homogenized (Red foil top)
The fat globules are broken up mechanically into fine particles, which remain distributed throughout the milk and do not rise to the surface. It is then pasteurized. It has the same fat content as pasteurized milk, but there is no creamline and it looks whiter. Because the fat globules are smaller, homogenized milk is more easily digested and is suitable for young children and invalids.
Storage time: 1–2 days in a cool larder. 2–3 days in a refrigerator.

Channel Island and South Devon (Gold foil top)
Milk from Jersey, Guernsey and South Devon breeds. Pasteurized. Because it contains more fat, it has a richer flavour and more creamy colour. The creamline shows clearly at the top of the bottle.
Storage time: 1–2 days in a cool larder. 2–3 days in a refrigerator.

Sterilized (Blue cap)
First homogenized, then bottled, sealed and heated above boiling point for 20–30 minutes. This treatment improves the keeping qualities

but gives it a caramel flavour. It has a rich creamy appearance and is sold in long slender necked bottles with crown caps. Makes excellent rice pudding, but junket will not set using this milk because of the heat treatment.
Storage time: unopened, at least 7 days without refrigeration, and several weeks is quite usual. Once opened, use as fresh milk.

Ultra heat treated (UHT)
Prepared from homogenized milk, it is heated to an extremely high temperature for 1 second only. Aseptically packed and sealed into foil lined containers. It has a slight caramel flavour. Excellent to keep in the store cupboard or use when camping.
Storage time: will keep for several months without refrigeration, providing the foil packet is not opened or damaged. Stamped with a 'use by' date. Once opened, use as fresh milk.

Untreated milk (Green foil top)
It is given no heat treatment and is bottled at the farm or dairy under a special licence issued by the Milk Marketing Board. Very clear cream-line. Only available locally. Untreated Channel Island and South Devon milk has a green foil cap with a gold stripe.
Storage time: 1 day in a cool larder. 2–3 days in a refrigerator.

Kosher (Blue and silver striped top) and
Kadassia (Purple and silver striped top)
These are usually pasteurized milks and are available in certain areas only. The colour code remains the same whether or not it is also Channel Island or homogenized milk. Untreated Kosher and Kadassia milk, in common with all other untreated milk, has a green top but is specifically labelled.
Storage time: pasteurized: 1–2 days in a cool larder. 2–3 days in a refrigerator.
Storage time: untreated: 1 day in a cool larder. 2–3 days in a refrigerator.

MILK IN SCOTLAND AND NORTHERN IRELAND

These have their own regulations regarding the sale of milk. In Scotland, most of the milk and cream is the same as that sold in England and Wales, but they have other types as well.

Premium (Green top with gold lattice) and
Standard (Plain green top) are untreated milks but certain quality and

safety standards are necessary. These milks are farm bottled.
Ordinary (Cerise top) is also a farm bottled milk. It is only sold in some sparsely populated rural areas and no special standard is required.

The regulations in Northern Ireland only allow pasteurized and farm bottled untreated milk to be produced. The identifying colours of the foil tops are the same as the rest of the UK. Whipping cream, double cream and sterilized cream are also produced, but the legislation does not cover UHT milk or cream, so none can be sold there. All milk and cream sold must have been produced on licensed farms in Northern Ireland, and bottles and cartons must be stamped with the date of delivery.

Light milk This milk is a newcomer to the British market. It is a general term for milk which has had some of the butterfat removed; containing about a third to a half of that in ordinary milk. It is, therefore, much lower in calories. The flavour is no different but there are less Vitamins A and D present. This milk is UHT treated.
Storage time: stamped with a 'use by' date. Once opened, use as fresh milk.

Skimmed milk This is the residue left after cream making. Because it contains little or no fat, it is low in calories but lacks Vitamins A and D. Skimmed milk is sometimes flavoured with chocolate or fruit and can be UHT treated.
Storage time: 1–2 days in a cool larder. 2–3 days in a refrigerator.

Buttermilk Was originally the residue liquid left after making butter, but is now a cultured product made in a similar way to yogurt. Skimmed milk is pasteurized and then special bacteria are added which produce the refreshing, mildly sour taste enjoyed by many. It has the same nutritional content as skimmed milk. Sold in cartons.
Storage time: stamped with a 'sell by' date. 2–3 days in the refrigerator or larder.

Evaporated milk Can be made from either skimmed or full cream milk. During manufacture, about two-thirds of the water content are removed by evaporation, it is then canned and sterilized. Evaporated milk has a mild caramel flavour. Although no sugar is added, because of its high concentration it tastes slightly sweet. This milk is not recommended for feeding babies.
Storage time: unopened, 3 months in a cool dry larder. Once opened, use as fresh.

Condensed milk Made from both skimmed and full cream milk. The water content is reduced by evaporation and the milk is sweetened. The finished product contains over 50 per cent sugar. This milk is not suitable for babies because of the high sugar content.
Storage time: unopened, 12 months in a cool dry larder. Once opened, because of the low water and high sugar content, it will keep longer than fresh milk but use within a few days.

Dried milk This is made from skimmed milk in 2 ways. The water can be evaporated by running the milk over hot rollers, or by spraying it into a hot steam of air. Spray dried milk is easiest to reconstitute and has a flavour nearer to fresh milk. It has the same nutritional value as fresh skimmed milk. Some dried milk has vegetable fat added to it and is sometimes enriched with Vitamins A and D. Dried skimmed milk must not be given to babies as it is nutritionally inadequate for them.
Storage time: air, damp and heat will cause deterioration but if kept in a tightly sealed container in a cool place, it will keep for up to 6 months. Once reconstituted, use as fresh milk.

Baby milks These are spray dried and modified to give varying amounts of fat to suit the age and feeding pattern of babies and to make it as near as possible to natural breast milk. It is also fortified with extra A and D vitamins and iron. Baby milk is made under sterile conditions and put into sterile packs. Care should be taken to use the milk at the correct strength. The milk must be measured accurately as too much is as bad for a baby as too little.
Storage time: keep the inner lining and outer wrapping tightly closed. Under no circumstances empty the powder into another container, as this could increase the risk of contamination. Keep in a cool dry cupboard. Once opened, it must be used within 3 weeks.

Cream

Cream is made from fresh milk and contains the fat with some of the other nutrients. There are many types of cream on the market and each one has a different amount of fat. These amounts are controlled by law.

Fresh dairy cream is pasteurized before it is packed into containers. Keep it cool, the refrigerator is the best place, and away from other foods which impart their flavour to it. When whipping, make sure that the cream and utensils are really cold. In hot weather or in a hot kitchen, stand the bowl over iced water. Do not overwhip or the cream will turn to butter and be of no use.

Half cream or Coffee cream Has 12 per cent fat content. Use as a pouring cream in coffee or on fruit. It will not whip.
Storage time: in the refrigerator, 2–3 days in summer, 3–4 days in winter.

Single cream Has at least 18 per cent fat content. Use as a pouring cream in coffee or on puddings and fruit. Add to soups and sauces. Will not whip. Also sold frozen in packets.
Storage time: in the refrigerator, 2–3 days in summer, 3–4 days in winter. Frozen cream, 3–4 months in a freezer.

Whipping cream Has 35 per cent fat content. Can also be bought frozen in blocks, or in pieces which can be used a few at a time. It can be whipped to twice its volume and piped on to cakes, pastries and puddings. Make certain frozen cream is completely defrosted before it is whipped.
Storage time: in the refrigerator, 2–3 days in summer, 3–4 days in winter. Frozen cream, 3–4 months in a freezer.

Double cream Has 48 per cent fat content. A rich pouring cream, excellent for whipping. For the best results, add 1 tablespoon milk to every 150 ml/$\frac{1}{4}$ pint cream. Double cream will float on top of soups and coffee.
Storage time: in the refrigerator, 2–3 days in summer, 3–4 days in winter. Frozen cream, 3–4 months in a freezer.

Thick double cream Has 48 per cent fat content. A very thick rich cream. It is too thick to pour and will not whip, so spoon it over fruit or puddings.
Storage time: in the refrigerator, 2–3 days in summer, 3–4 days in winter. Frozen cream, 3–4 months in a freezer.

Extended life double cream Has 48 per cent fat content. The milk is heated and vacuum sealed into bottles. A thick cream to be spooned. Can be lightly whipped.
Storage time: 2–3 weeks in the refrigerator. Once opened, use as fresh cream.

Clotted cream Has 55 per cent fat content or more. For this cream,

the milk is heated to simmering point and then cooled for about $4\frac{1}{2}$ hours. The thick cream crust is skimmed off and packed into cartons. It has its own special flavour and colour, and spreads like butter. Traditional in the west country with scones and jam, it is also delicious with fruit, cakes and pastries.
Storage time: in the refrigerator, 2–3 days in summer, 3–4 days in winter.

Ultra heat treated (UHT) cream Half cream, single and whipping cream are treated and packed in the same way as milk. Use as fresh cream.
Storage time: unopened, 6 weeks without refrigeration. Once opened, use as fresh cream.

Soured cream A specially cultured single cream. Excellent for cooking and salad dressings. It cannot be made in the home from pasteurized fresh cream. However, you can make acidulated cream by adding a little lemon juice to fresh cream. This will thicken it and give a mild acid taste. Use in place of soured cream in recipes.
Storage time: 3–4 days in the refrigerator or cool place. Stamped with a 'sell by' date.

Sterilized half cream Has 12 per cent fat content. It is homogenized then filled into cans, sealed and sterilized. A pouring cream with a mild caramel flavour.
Storage time: unopened, up to 2 years in a cool dry larder. Once opened, use as fresh cream.

Sterilized cream Has 23 per cent fat content. Treated in the same way as sterilized half cream. It is thicker and has a stronger caramel flavour. It can be spooned but not whipped.
Storage time: unopened, up to 2 years in a cool dry larder. Once opened, use as fresh cream.

Yogurt

Yogurt is a soured milk product thought to have originated among the nomadic tribes of Eastern Europe. It was traditionally a drink, made by allowing milk to ferment and turn acid. Today, yogurt is made commercially from a skimmed milk base to which extra skimmed milk powder is added. A special culture is added to the milk, which is kept under controlled conditions until it has reached the required acidity and consistency. It is then cooled, flavoured and packaged.

Types of yogurt

Fat free yogurt contains less than 0·5 per cent milk fat.
Low fat yogurt contains no more than 1.5 per cent milk fat.
Whole fruit or *real fruit* contain whole or broken fruit in a sugar syrup.
Fruit flavoured has a fruit juice syrup added.

Storage and care of yogurt

Always buy yogurt from a refrigerated cabinet and see that the date stamp has not expired. Keep in the refrigerator and eat within 5–7 days. If it is stored at room temperature, it will become more acid and will eventually separate. Commercially frozen yogurt can be kept in a freezer for 1 month. Do not freeze any other type as it will separate when thawed.

Food value

Yogurt contains the same nutrients as skimmed milk and because of the extra milk powder which was added during manufacture, it is a good source of protein and the B group vitamin, riboflavin. As it contains little fat, it is deficient in Vitamins A and D but these are now added to many brands. Fruit flavoured yogurt is high in sugar.

Making your own

It is easy to make your own yogurt, either in an electric yogurt maker or in a thermos flask. For the best results, use UHT milk and add a teaspoon or two of dried milk powder; this will make it thicker, as home-made yogurt tends to be thinner than the commercially produced ones. Warm the milk to blood heat, add some plain unpasteurized yogurt and pour into the container in the maker or into a thermos flask. Leave overnight and then chill.

Butter

Butter is made from cows' milk, taking 10 litres/18 pints to make 450 g/1 lb. Butter is a good source of Vitamin A but the amount of Vitamin D varies according to the amount of sunshine. There is a little calcium present. The British laws controlling the making of butter are strict, no colouring, preservatives or extra vitamins are allowed. Only salt can be added, this gives flavour and improves the keeping quality.

How butter is made
First of all the cream is separated from the milk. There are two ways of making butter and these processes produce butters with different flavours.

Sweet cream butter The cream is pasteurized. Before it is churned, it is allowed to age for about 12 hours in tanks which are kept at a low temperature. This butter is a golden yellow and, as the name implies, it has a sweet creamy taste.

Lactic butter The cream is kept at a temperature of about 20°C/65–70°F and the lactic acid is allowed to develop. This produces the substances which flavour the butter. Lactic butter is pale cream and has a fresh clean taste.

Salt can be added to both types of butter. They are both sold throughout the United Kingdom. Most of the butter made in this country is sweet cream. New Zealand and Eire also make this type. Lactic butter comes from Europe, mainly Denmark, The Netherlands and France, although they also make some sweet cream butter.

Storage
Keep in a cool dark place, the refrigerator is best, otherwise keep covered in a cool larder. To freeze butter, leave it in the original wrapping, put into a polythene bag or container and seal well. Unsalted butter will keep better than salted butter in the freezer.

Storage times in unopened packets:

In a cool larder	1–3 weeks depending on temperature
In a refrigerator	3–4 weeks
In a freezer	
salted	3 months
unsalted	6 months

Use opened packets as quickly as possible.

OTHER BUTTER PRODUCTS

Concentrated butter This butter, made especially for cooking, has been available on the Continent for many years and is now being made and sold in this country. It is processed by carefully melting the butter and then spinning it until virtually all the water is removed. It has a butterfat content of 99.8 per cent. Because it contains no salt or water and few of the milk solids, this butter is ideal for frying and can be used in place of clarified butter or ghee. It can be used for some baking, only half to three-quarters of the amount you would use with conventional butter is needed and more water must be added to the mixture. It is not suitable for spreading.

Low fat butter and margarine spreads These are made with butter and vegetable oils, and contain a greater amount of water than the 16 per cent allowed in butter or margarine. Therefore, they cannot be called by these names and are sold under trade names. They contain only half the calories of other fats but because of the high water content, they are unsuitable for frying. Generally, Vitamins A and D are added to give the same nutritional value as margarine.

Eggs

Eggs are a naturally packaged convenience food. They contain high quality protein, fat, iron, Vitamins A, D and B, in fact most of the nutrients essential for life, but are high in cholesterol. The yolk or shell

Old	New	
Large	Size 1	
		70 g
	Size 2	
		65 g
$2\frac{3}{16}$ oz	Size 3	
Standard		60 g
$1\frac{7}{8}$ oz	Size 4	
		55 g
Medium	Size 5	
$1\frac{5}{8}$ oz		50 g
Small	Size 6	
$1\frac{1}{2}$ oz		45 g
Extra small	Size 7	

colour makes no difference to the food value. The colour of the shell is determined by the breed.

All eggs must be graded for size and quality. They are graded according to weight with a range of 7 sizes. The largest is '1', the smallest is '7'. For the average recipe, use sizes 3 or 4.

The code number of the week the eggs were purchased must be given on all cartons of 6 eggs. The numbers begin with Week 1 at the beginning of the year through to Week 52 at the end of December. The EEC country where they were packed is coded. British packed are marked 9. There are codes, too, for the regions of the country where they were packed. The licence number of the packing station and the name and address of the packing or retailing company must be also printed on the carton.

Storage

Keep eggs in the carton, placed with pointed ends down so that the air space does not bear the weight of the egg. The ideal temperature is about 10°C/50°F. If kept in the refrigerator, store away from the ice box and strong smelling foods because the shell is porous and absorbs flavours. For boiling, they are best taken out of the refrigerator and left at room temperature overnight or at least 30 minutes before using.

The estimated storage life of eggs is:

In a cupboard in the kitchen	1 week
In a cold larder	2 weeks
In a refrigerator	3 weeks

All about fish.

Fish supplies depend on the weather and the luck and skill of the fisherman. Therefore, the supplies can vary from day to day and from week to week.

There are several points to bear in mind when looking for fresh, good quality fish at a sensible price. Appearance as well as smell will tell you whether it is in good condition. Whole fish should have shiny protruding eyes with clear black centres, bright red gills, fresh colour, glistening scales and some natural slime. The flesh should be firm, not soft and floppy. In deciding which fish to buy, remember that there is more waste on some fish than others; the price for fillets will be higher than the price of whole fish, but there is little waste. Whole plaice or herring lose about half their weight in filleting.

Is it good food value?
Just like meat, fish is a body building food. Oily fish, such as mackerel and herring, contains a considerable amount of Vitamin D. This is essential for growing children and the elderly, if they are to have strong, healthy bones. It is also an important food during pregnancy and breastfeeding. For the weight conscious, white fish is a good choice, as this has practically no fat and is low in calories. Fish also contains iron, iodine and some of the B vitamins.

Storage and preparation

Ideally, buy fish on the day it is needed. Try to keep it in a cool place until the fish can be put, loosely wrapped, in the upper part of the refrigerator. Store for up to 24 hours.

If you buy frozen fish, keep it well chilled in an insulated bag, or wrapped in layers of newspaper, until it can be placed in the frozen food compartment of the refrigerator or in the freezer. Do not allow to defrost.

In a refrigerator Commercially frozen fish can be kept for a limited time in the freezer compartment depending on the star rating of the refrigerator. Check the package instructions.

In a freezer Flavour deteriorates if fish is stored for too long. Oily fish eventually tastes rancid. The fish must be firmly wrapped in polythene or similar covering, sealed and kept at a temperature of −18°C/0°F or below.

For the best results, keep white fish no longer than 6 months, and oily fish, smoked fish, shellfish and cooked fish dishes for a maximum of 3 months. After these times, the fish is still safe to eat but the flavour slowly spoils and the fish loses its fresh taste. Be careful to wrap it thoroughly as 'freezer burn', which will appear on any unwrapped parts, makes the fish become tough and inedible. This is because it is exposed to the drying effect of the freezer.

Fish can be cooked and then frozen. This is satisfactory for poached fish in a sauce, like sole florentine or fish provençale.

Thawing

Unless fish is already coated in batter or egg and breadcrumbs ready to fry, it should be defrosted slowly in the refrigerator to get the best results. This allows the fish to cook more evenly; if it is cooked when still frozen there is a tendency to over cook the outside of the fish before it is cooked through to the centre. In an emergency, small fish or fillets can be cooked from frozen but allow extra time. For large fish such as salmon, it is essential to defrost fully before cooking. Once any fish has been partially or completely thawed, it must never be refrozen.

Cleaning

Wash sea fish under running cold water. Freshwater fish can be soaked in several changes of cold salt water if it is muddy. If the fish has not been prepared by the fishmonger, you will need to clean the fish. Remove the innards and fins, if it is not to be skinned any scales should be quickly scraped off. Dover sole is skinned before it is filleted but other fish have the skin taken off afterwards. Salmon skin is peeled off after cooking.

Flat fish are filleted into 2 or 4 fillets; herring, mackerel and whiting can be boned and left whole. Large fish like cod are filleted by the fishmonger and sold in fillets, or cutlets and steaks – slices cut across the body including the bone.

Best times for buying

The quality of fish varies with the seasons. Each fish has a spawning time, when the eggs are produced, and less should be caught at this time. Immediately after spawning the flesh is softer and not so good for eating. The chart shows approximately when fish should be at their best. There may be as much as 2 months difference in the season for fish caught off the south coast and those caught later off the north of Scotland. However, herring are first caught off the Shetland Islands and later in the year they are caught further south.

	JAN	FEB	MAR	APR	MAY	JUN	JUL	AUG	SEP	OCT	NOV	DEC
FISH												
Bass	■	■	■					■	■	■	■	■
Brill	■	■				■	■	■	■	■	■	■
Carp	■	■	■	■						■	■	■
Cockles	■	■	■	■						■	■	■
Cod	■	■				■	■	■	■	■	■	■
Conger eel	■	■								■	■	■
Crab				■	■	■	■	■	■	■	■	■
Crawfish				■	■	■	■	■	■			
Crayfish	■	■	■	■					■	■	■	■
Dab	■	■				■	■	■	■	■	■	■
Dogfish (huss, flake, rigg)	■	■	■	■	■	■				■	■	■
Dover sole					■	■	■	■	■	■	■	
Dublin Bay prawns	■	■	■	■	■	■	■	■	■	■	■	■
Eel	■	■	■	■	■	■	■	■	■	■	■	■
Flounder	■	■			■	■	■	■	■	■	■	
Grey mullet	■	■							■	■	■	■
Gurnard	■	■	■	■			■	■	■	■	■	■
Haddock	■						■	■	■	■	■	■
Hake	■					■	■	■	■	■	■	■
Halibut	■					■	■	■	■	■	■	■
Herring	■	■					■	■	■	■	■	■

	JAN	FEB	MAR	APR	MAY	JUN	JUL	AUG	SEP	OCT	NOV	DEC
John Dory	■	■	■	■								
Lemon sole	■	■	■					■	■	■	■	■
Ling	■	■	■					■	■	■	■	■
Lobster				■	■	■	■	■	■	■	■	
Mackerel	■	■	■	■	■	■	■	■	■	■	■	■
Megrim	■	■	■					■	■	■	■	■
Monkfish	■	■	■	■	■	■	■	■	■	■	■	■
Mussels	■	■								■	■	■
Oysters	■	■	■							■	■	■
Pilchards	■	■				■	■	■	■	■	■	■
Plaice	■				■	■	■	■	■	■	■	■
Prawns	■	■	■	■	■	■	■	■	■	■	■	■
Redfish	■	■	■	■	■	■	■	■	■	■	■	■
Red mullet					■	■	■	■	■			
Rockfish		■	■	■	■	■	■					
Saithe (Coley)		■	■	■				■	■	■		
Salmon		■	■	■	■	■	■	■	■			
Farmed salmon	■	■	■	■	■				■	■	■	■
Salmon trout				■	■	■	■					
Sardine	■	■				■	■	■	■	■	■	■
Scallop	■	■	■						■	■	■	■
Seabream	■	■				■	■	■	■	■	■	■
Shrimp		■	■	■	■	■	■	■	■	■		
Skate	■	■			■	■	■	■	■	■	■	■
Smelt	■	■	■				■	■	■	■	■	■
Sprat	■	■	■							■	■	■
Squid					■	■	■	■	■	■		
Trout – brown				■	■	■	■	■	■			
– rainbow	■	■	■	■	■	■	■	■	■	■	■	■
Turbot					■	■	■	■	■	■		
Whelk				■	■	■	■	■				
Whitebait		■	■	■	■	■	■					
Winkle	■	■	■	■						■	■	■
Witch	■	■	■	■				■	■	■	■	■

Ways to cook fish

Fish can be cooked by grilling, baking, frying, boiling, poaching, braising and steaming. It is quick to cook; a useful fact to remember when you want a speedy meal.

Grilling A fast and simple method of cooking which gives a good flavour. Fillets, cutlets and small whole fish can be cooked in this way. The prepared fish is seasoned, brushed with a little oil or melted butter and can, if liked, be sprinkled with dried breadcrumbs. Round fish should be slashed across with 2–3 cuts to enable heat to penetrate more quickly. Preheat the grill before the fish is put under and grease the grill rack. Alternatively, cover the rack with greased foil. Cook the fish fairly slowly until it is tender, turning it once, then turn the grill up high during the last few minutes to brown. Serve with lemon quarters to garnish and squeeze over, or a mouth-watering savoury herb-flavoured butter.

Barbecues are a way of grilling. Brush the fish with oil and wrap in foil, or use a double sided wire barbecue grid to hold the fish.

Baking This is a good way to cook when you want to avoid cooking smells. Butter an ovenproof dish and put the fish in, season and cover. Whole fish can be filled loosely with a savoury stuffing and then sewn up or secured with a skewer. Fish cutlets can also be filled with a tasty stuffing and put in a buttered dish. Dot with knobs of butter or pour over a little milk and cook until tender.

Frying There are two ways of frying fish, either in shallow fat, usually butter or oil or a mixture, or in a pan of deep fat.

Shallow frying Dip the prepared fish into milk, then into well-seasoned flour. With butter in the frying pan foaming hot, cook the fish first on one side and then on the other until golden brown. Sprinkle with lemon juice and chopped fresh parsley, and serve as soon as possible. The temperature of the fat is important. If it is too cool, the fish will be greasy and soggy. If too hot, it may burn the outside coating. Allow extra time for frozen seafoods.

Deep frying Plaice, whiting, smelts, whitebait, whole sole or fillets, pieces of huss, hake, cod, coley and haddock can all be cooked in this way. It is not a suitable method for really thick pieces of fish. The fish must have a coating to protect it from the hot fat; this is usually either egg and breadcrumbs or a light batter. Ready breadcrumbed or batter-coated seafoods should be deep fried straight from the freezer. Suitable fats for frying include cooking fats, lard and vegetable oils. Some shellfish can also be coated in egg and breadcrumbs or batter. These include scallops, mussels and prawns.

Poaching Fish is poached in gently simmering liquid; this allows the fish to cook without breaking up, as it will do if cooked too fiercely. Fish is never actually boiled, although the word is used in some recipes.

The liquid used may be water (sometimes with wine or vinegar added) or milk flavoured with vegetables, herbs and seasoning. The cooking time for fish is too short to develop the full flavour from these ingredients, so a 'court bouillon' is often made, and the fish cooked in it. This is simply a well flavoured liquid which may be wine or vinegar and water, with onion, carrot, leek or celery, herbs and seasoning, boiled together for 15–20 minutes and then cooled before the fish is poached in it. Fish can be poached either in a covered dish in the oven or in a pan on top of the cooker. Large fish such as salmon can be cooked in a fish kettle or in a roasting tin in the oven, well covered with foil. The cooking liquor is generally used to make a well flavoured sauce to serve with the fish.

Braising Butter the bottom of a suitably sized pan and put in a layer of sliced onion and carrot. Lay the fish on top, pour around fish stock or wine and water to come halfway up the sides, and braise gently until cooked. Use the strained liquor, thickened with beurre manié, to make a sauce.

Steaming A useful way to cook a few fillets of fish or 1 or 2 slices. The flavour of the fish is concentrated and the fish keeps a good texture. Serve with a little lemon juice sprinkled over, or pour a parsley or anchovy sauce around. For cooking times see page 184.

How to tell when fish is cooked

Fish changes in appearance as it cooks. The translucent flesh becomes opaque and white or pink, depending on type. If it is being poached, you also see a creamy substance flaking into the liquid. When the fish is cooked and ready to eat, it flakes easily and will come away cleanly from the bone.

Cooking and serving fish

Here are some suggestions for cooking and serving both the familiar and less well known types of fish. A star ★ shows which are frozen commercially.

FISH	SERVING SUGGESTIONS
Bass Sea fish. Steel grey back with silvery underside. Delicate flesh. *Grill, bake, fry, poach, braise.*	Poach, drain and serve with anchovy butter or hollandaise sauce. Serve cold like salmon.
Brill Sea fish. Upper side fawny brown with a flecked pattern. Whitish underside. Sold whole, weighing 750 g–1 kg/1½–2 lb, or in fillets. *Bake, shallow fry, grill, braise.*	Poach in a little white wine or cider. Thicken the sauce with beurre manié; use 40 g/1½ oz butter mixed with 25 g/1 oz flour to 300 ml/½ pint liquid.
Carp Freshwater fish. Carp is farmed successfully. These fish have few scales and a good texture and flavour. About 1.25–1.5 kg/2½–3 lb in weight, serves 4–5. *Poach or bake whole, fry, grill.*	Soak in water, with a little vinegar added, for 30 minutes. Poach in court bouillon or red wine with carrot, onion and herbs. Make a sauce from the liquor.
Cockles★ Shellfish. A clam-like shellfish with a ribbed shell. Keep in a bucket of sea water for several hours before using, to clean them. Supply likely to be short in stormy weather. *Boil.*	These are eaten raw or cooked. May be made into cockle pie, or cooked like mussels, with cream and served as cockles in cream. Can be bought pickled.
Cod★ Sea fish. A large fish, so sold in fillets, steaks or cutlets. White flesh with grey skin. Fillets: *Fry, poach, steam.* Cutlets: *Stuff and bake.* Steaks: *Bake, poach, shallow fry, grill.*	Casserole 'à la provençale' with onion, tomato and white wine. Make into fish pies, fish cakes, croquettes etc. If steamed or poached, serve with a well flavoured sauce, such as parsley.

FISH	SERVING SUGGESTIONS
Coley (Saithe)* Sea fish. Flesh is pinkish grey, slightly coarse in texture. Sold in fillets and steaks. *Poach, fry.*	Satisfactory for made up dishes such as fish pie; mix cooked flaked fish with white sauce and arrange in layers with sliced hard-boiled egg and tomato. Brown the top.
Conger eel (Sea eel) Sea fish. A lengthy eel with blue grey and white skin. Sold in steaks. Firm flesh. Supply is irregular. *Stew, bake.*	Used in soups such as the Breton cotriade, which is made with a mixture of fish cooked with potatoes and herbs. Can be made into a fish curry or fish pies.
Crab* Shellfish. May be bought alive but are more often sold ready cooked in this country. Can be fresh or frozen, whole or prepared. Should be relatively heavy for their size. Remove the gills known as the dead men's fingers, and bony stomach sac. *Boil.*	White meat comes from the legs, claws and body; brown meat from the shell. Dressed crab is served in the clean shell. Popular in salads and sandwiches. Use also for hot dishes, risotto, 'au gratin' and crab soup.
Crawfish* Shellfish. Large shellfish similar to lobster, but a dull brownish red colour and without the large claws. *Boil.*	Similar to lobster. Tail meat is used. Treat as lobster for hot or cold dishes.
Crayfish Shellfish. When these small freshwater shellfish are boiled, they turn scarlet. *Boil.*	Cook in court bouillon for about 12 minutes. Serve unshelled. Classic garnish for poulet sauté marengo.
Dab Sea fish. Look like small plaice without the spots, but is actually a different fish. Some too small for filleting, so cooked whole. *Fry, steam, bake, grill.*	Grill and serve with a savoury butter. Bake for 15 minutes and coat with a home-made tomato sauce.

FISH	SERVING SUGGESTIONS
Dogfish Sea fish. Also called huss, flake or rigg. Unusual in that it has no bones, only a gristly spine. Sold skinned. Round with pink flesh. When stale, smells of ammonia. *Deep fry, poach, steam.*	Dip in batter and deep fry. Excellent poached or steamed and served with a sauce, such as tomato.
Dublin Bay prawns* Shellfish. The Italian name of scampi is normally used. In France, they are called langoustines, Norway lobster is another name. Usually shelled. *Deep fry, poach.*	Poach and put in a seafood cocktail or flan. Dip in batter, deep fry and serve with a sweet sour sauce.
Eel Migratory. A long snake like fish which migrates to the Sargasso sea to spawn. The young are sold as elvers. Often sold alive. Skin before cooking. *Stew, boil, fry.*	Jellied eels and eel pie are British traditions. In France, they are cooked 'en matelote' casseroled in red wine, or fried and then cooked with sorrel and spinach.
Flounder Sea fish. A flat fish with a dark skin on top. Underneath it is white, sometimes with spots. *Fry, grill, poach.*	Can be cut into smallish pieces, dipped in batter and deep fried. Serve with chips and tartare sauce, or with a sweet sour sauce and rice.
Grey mullet Sea fish. A silvery blue grey fish with fairly large scales. One fish serves 3–4. Rather like mackerel, but with a less rich flavour. *Bake, fry, poach, stew.*	Cut in steaks and cook in a casserole with onion, tomato, herbs and a glass of wine. Poach and coat with mushroom or anchovy sauce.
Gurnard Sea fish. There are grey, yellow and red varieties of gurnard. They have a large head and distinctive fins. The flesh is white and firm. *Poach, bake.*	Poach in court bouillon. Drain then cover with a cheese sauce, with a little cream added. Sprinkle with grated cheese and brown. Use in soups.

FISH	SERVING SUGGESTIONS
Haddock* Sea fish. Recognize haddock by the black line down the length of the body and the black 'thumb' print behind the head. Small haddock are sold whole, others are filleted. *Poach, fry, bake.*	Serve with cheese or mushroom sauce. Poach in beer and make a sauce with the cooking liquor. Fry in batter. Stuff small fish and bake whole.
Hake* Sea fish. Grey back shading to silver then white. Tender flaky flesh. Whole ones weigh about 450 g–1 kg/1–2 lb. Buy fillets, cutlets or large pieces. *Grill, shallow fry in slices, poach.*	As the flesh is rather like cod, use in the same recipes. Grill the steaks and serve with fennel flavoured sauce.
Halibut* Sea fish. A large fish with firm white flesh. Sold in steaks or fillets. *Poach, bake, shallow fry, grill.*	Any recipe for sole or turbot can be adapted for this fish. Cover the bottom of flameproof dish with a purée of mushrooms, put poached halibut on top and pour over a cheese sauce. Brown under the grill.
Herring* Sea fish. Bright silvery fish with red eyes and gills. Average weight 150–350 g/6–12 oz. Buy whole or filleted. Serves 1 per person. *Grill, shallow fry, bake.*	Coat in oatmeal and fry in bacon fat. Stuff and bake. Souse in vinegar and water. The roe can be fried, poached or made into a pâté.
John Dory Sea fish. A strange looking fish with delicate white flesh. No regular supply, but caught off the south coast sometimes. Sold filleted. *Poach, fry, grill, braise.*	Cook in the same way as sole or turbot. Good poached with a cream sauce. Fry in butter and serve on a bed of tomato flavoured risotto.
Ling Sea fish. A moderately large fish, sold in fillets or steaks. *Bake, grill, fry, poach.*	Cook in the same way as cod. A good choice for fish moulds, served with shrimp sauce.

FISH	SERVING SUGGESTIONS
Lobster* Shellfish. Sold live or cooked. Blue black when alive, they change to red when cooked. Large front claws. Should be heavy in proportion for its size; the tail should be springy. White incrustations are to be avoided as they are a sign of age. Best size between 450 g–1 kg/1–2 lb. *Boil, grill.*	Lobster, boiled and served cold with salad, is a summer luxury. Hot lobster dishes can be grilled, or the poached lobster flesh removed from the shell and gently reheated in a sauce. Lobster thermidor, for instance, flavoured with herbs, shallots and mustard.
Mackerel* Sea fish. Blue green with wavy black markings. Silvery underside. Sold whole or filleted. Weighing 225–450 g/8 oz–1 lb. *Grill, bake, shallow fry.*	Grill and serve with gooseberry sauce in summer, or in other seasons with mustard sauce. For soused mackerel, fillet the fish, then roll and cook in a vinegar marinade with shallots and herbs. Serve cold.
Monkfish Sea fish. Also called anglerfish. About one third of the length is taken up by a large ugly head, but it is the tail meat which is eaten. This has a firm white flesh. *Poach, bake, fry, grill.*	Poach and serve hot with a sauce or use cold in a fish salad. Firm enough to make kebabs. Can be an ingredient of bourride, the provençale fish soup served with garlic mayonnaise.
Mussels* Shellfish. Sold alive in the shell, by the pint or more often by weight. Allow 450 g/1 lb per person. Wash throughly in several changes of water. Discard any broken or open mussels; they should close when tapped. *Boil.*	Moules marinière is a great favourite. Boil mussels in white wine or cider with shallot or onion, bouquet garni and a few peppercorns. They can also be eaten with garlic butter, added to a seafood risotto or made into soup.
Oysters Shellfish. The most expensive shellfish. Sold by the dozen. Open just before serving. Holding with	Eaten raw as an appetizer, freshly opened and served in the half shell with natural juices, on ice. Brown

FISH	SERVING SUGGESTIONS
Oysters cont. a cloth, use an oyster knife to separate the two shells and cut the muscle free. Or use a short, wide-bladed knife. Allow 6–12 per person. *Poach, fry.*	bread and butter with lemon accompany them. Can also be poached or fried as oyster fritters.
Pilchards Sea fish. These small silvery fish are caught off the Cornish and Devon coasts. Small pilchards are sardines. *Grill, fry, souse.*	Star gazy pie is a Cornish tradition, made with the heads of the pilchards peeping out from under a light pie crust.
Plaice* Sea fish. The spots of dull orange or yellow identify this flat fish. Grey brown upper side and white underneath. Sold whole or filleted. Fillets can be skinned before cooking. *Fry, grill, poach.*	An unusual and delicious way to serve these is to stuff and bake. Cut the flesh away from the backbone to make a pocket. Fill with a savoury stuffing and bake. Garnish with prawns and lemon.
Prawns* Shellfish. Sold boiled, ready to eat, in shells or peeled. 450 g/1 lb whole prawns gives about 225 g/8 oz shelled flesh. *Boil.*	Prawn cocktails are always popular. Also good in seafood salads. Can be made into a mild curry. Prawn bisque can be made using the shells as flavouring and the flesh as garnish.
Redfish Sea fish. Also called Norway haddock. With reddish orange colour on the back, this plump fish is sold in fillets. Remove sharp spines. *Fry, grill, bake.*	Stuff and bake using any recipe for stuffed haddock. Fillets can be fried in butter, grilled and served with a savoury butter, or deep fried.
Red mullet* Sea fish. Sold whole. Weight 175–225 g/6–8 oz. Pinkish red back and silvery belly. Sold frozen; fresh fish available in summer. *Grill, bake, fry.*	Remove the tough scales and spiky fins. Often cooked ungutted. Bake 'en papillote' wrapped in a parcel of foil or greaseproof paper and baked in the oven. Excellent for a barbecue.

FISH	SERVING SUGGESTIONS
Rockfish (Catfish) Sea fish. A large fish sold in fillets. *Fry, bake, grill.*	Cook, using any recipe recommended for cod.
Salmon* Migratory. Silver grey colour with glistening scales. Pink flesh. Sold whole, weighing 3–13 kg/7–30 lb, or in steaks and cutlets. Scotch salmon, 1st February – 15th September. Irish from 1st January. Farmed salmon are in good supply and weigh from 1.75–6 kg/4–13 lb. Frozen ones are imported from Canada and Japan. *Poach, bake, braise, grill.*	Poach in court bouillon. If you do not have a large enough fish kettle, cook in a roasting tin surrounded with liquid and covered with foil. Skin after cooking. Serve hot with hollandaise sauce, or cold with mayonnaise and cucumber salad. Use trimmings or a tail section to make a mousse.
Salmon trout* Migratory. Similar in appearance to a small salmon. Those sold in the fishmongers usually weigh between 750 g–1.75 kg/1½–4 lb. Maximum size can be about 6.75 kg/15 lb. Pale pink moist flesh with a good flavour and excellent texture. *Poach, bake.*	Poach in court bouillon. Cool, drain, skin and serve with mayonnaise and salad for a special summer meal. Glaze with aspic for a party dish.
Scallops* Shellfish. Sold singly in the shell or frozen by weight. Smaller 'Queen' variety also sold frozen, or occasionally can be found fresh. Remove black parts, wash well to remove sand. *Poach, fry, grill.*	Poach and serve in a sauce made from the cooking liquor. Bacon, garlic and mushrooms are flavours that blend well with them. May be coated in egg and breadcrumbs and grilled on kebab skewers.
Sea bream* Sea fish. Red fins with a dull red back, silvery belly and sides. Weight 750 g–1 kg/1½–2 lb. Usually sold whole. Wash, scale and clean. *Grill, bake.*	The whole fish can be stuffed and baked. A mixture of chopped cooked onion, mushrooms and parsley bound with fresh breadcrumbs makes a good filling.

FISH	SERVING SUGGESTIONS
Shrimps* Shellfish. Small, but delicious, pink and brown shrimps are cooked and sold in the shell by weight. Used to be sold by the pint. *Boil.*	Potted shrimps are covered with butter which is flavoured with mace. Often sold frozen. Warm sufficiently to melt the butter and eat with hot toast. Fresh shrimps make good soups and sauces.
Skate Sea fish. The triangular wings of this fish are sold whole or in portions. *Poach, fry.*	Cut the ribbed flesh into portions. Poach, drain and fry in hot browned butter. Sprinkle with a little vinegar and a few capers before serving.
Smelt Sea fish. These delicate little fish are also called sparling. Small silvery fish with white flesh. *Grill, fry, bake.*	Coat with egg and breadcrumbs, thread on to skewers and deep fry. Grill and serve with a savoury butter.
Sole - Dover* Sea fish. One of the best flat fish. Oval shape with dull grey brown skin which can be pulled off the whole fish. Weight about 450 g/1 lb. Buy whole or filleted. Cook small slip soles, weighing 175–225 g/6–8 oz whole. *Poach, fry, bake, steam, grill.*	Cookery books have many recipes for sole, most of these can be successfully adapted for other white fish. Sole colbert can only be prepared with dover sole as it needs to be skinned whole.
Sole - Lemon Sea fish. Not quite the excellence of Dover sole, but a useful substitute. Slightly broader with a yellow tinge to the skin. *Poach, fry, bake, steam, grill.*	Poach and serve with a Veronique garnish of white wine sauce with grapes. Make into any of the classic sole dishes. Fry or grill and serve with a savoury butter or tomato sauce.

FISH	SERVING SUGGESTIONS
Sprats Sea fish. Small silvery fish about 10–13 cm/4–5 inches in length. Buy by weight. *Grill, shallow fry.*	As these are an oily fish, they need not be brushed with oil before grilling. Garnish with lemon quarters. For frying, dip in milk and then flour; brown in butter and oil.
Squid* These have a long greyish body with tentacles and a head. There are two triangular fins on the side of the body. Small squid are tender enough to slice and fry. Any over 15 cm/6 inches in length need to be stuffed whole or sliced and stewed until tender. *Fry, stew.*	Pull the head and tentacles away from the body. Put aside the ink sac if needed for a sauce. Discard the head and the transparent skeletal piece in the tail. Cut off the skin the fins and tentacles. Wash well. Dip in batter and fry. Casserole larger squid with tomatoes, onion and garlic.
Trout* Freshwater fish. Brown trout inhabit streams, rivers and lakes. Rainbow trout are farmed and these are generally on sale. Weight 225–275 g/8–10 oz. *Fry, poach, grill.*	Scale, clean and wash, then dip in milk followed by seasoned flour. Fry in butter. When cooked on one side, turn and add a few almonds to brown with the fish. Excellent for a barbecue.
Turbot Sea fish. A large flat fish usually sold in fillets. Smaller ones, weighing 750 g–1 kg/$1\frac{1}{2}$–2 lb are called chicken turbot. Fish farming is being developed to produce these. *Poach, bake, steam, braise, grill.*	As turbot is a white fish, the fillets can be cooked in similar ways to sole, though cooking times are a fraction longer. Poach and drain, then put on a bed of cooked chopped spinach and coat with a cheese sauce for turbot à la florentine.
Whelks Shellfish. Larger than winkles with a pointed shell. Sold cooked. The large muscular foot is the part usually eaten. *Boil, steam.*	Inclined to be rather chewy, but a splendid flavour. Shellfish addicts enjoy a platter of seafoods such as whelks, cockles, prawns and shrimps. Add to seafood cocktails or risotto.

FISH	SERVING SUGGESTIONS
Whitebait* Sea fish. These tiny silvery fish are young herrings, often with junior sprats mixed in as well. Buy by weight. *Deep fry.*	An English delicacy. They became a tradition in the last century when whitebait swam up the Thames. Dip in milk and coat with flour. Deep fry until crisp and brown, and eat whole served with lemon quarters.
Winkles Shellfish. Usually sold boiled and in the shell. If uncooked, wash well and soak to get rid of sand, then boil for 5 minutes. *Boil.*	Still to be found on shellfish stalls, as well as at the fishmongers. They are 'winkled' out of the shell with a pin, sprinkled with vinegar and eaten with brown bread and butter. Make into sandwiches or put on a platter of assorted seafoods.

All about meat.

Value for money is important, especially in the purchasing of meat. Economical buying means not only recognizing good quality but also knowing which cut to use.

Buying the right cut

Generally speaking, the best cuts of meat come from the hind part of the animal, as the muscles in this part of the body do less work and are therefore more tender. This is shown in the texture of the meat, particularly beef which is older and much larger than lamb, veal and pork. The prime quality cuts suitable for grilling, frying and roasting have a fine grain and little or no gristle or the gelatinous sinews known as 'connective tissue'. Meat with a coarser grain and a lot of connective tissue must be cooked by a slow moist method e.g. casseroling and pot-roasting, if it is to be good to eat.

Choosing for quality

Even knowing which cut to buy, how is it possible to tell which meat is tender and has a good flavour? Firstly, try to buy meat from a butcher or shop with a consistently high standard. It will have been his responsibility to 'hang' or 'age' beef, lamb and veal so that the flesh can relax and become more tender. The flavour of the meat will also develop. Secondly, much can be learnt from the appearance of the meat.

Although by law, nothing can be added to meat to alter the colour, it can vary quite considerably according to the breed and age of the animal, and how the meat was stored and packed. Even the light shining on pre-packed meat in the storage cabinet in the supermarket will give the meat a different appearance. Look for meat which has a clear colour with no blotches or dry patches. The flesh and fat should look firm not flabby, and moist but not sticky, and with no beads of moisture showing on the surface of the meat. The fat should look clean with no sign that it has absorbed or been lying in any blood; this would give the fat a pink tinge. However, do remember that it is difficult to identify the colour or quality of frozen meat. Therefore, when buying ready frozen meat, one must rely on the reputation of the supplier.

Lamb

Just about half the lamb consumed in this country is home produced, and the remainder is mostly imported from New Zealand. Good quality meat is lean and firm, with a fine grain. The colour is pink, deepening to a dull red as the season progresses. The fat is creamy white. There should be little difference in the colour of New Zealand lamb, although the fat may be a little creamier.

It is good to eat at all times, but the young lamb at the start of the season has an especially sweet taste. The new season for home produced lamb starts about March or April and although it is delicious to eat, it is expensive at this time. It is at its cheapest and most abundant in the late summer and early autumn, so this is the time to buy home-produced lamb for your freezer. The new young lamb from New Zealand comes into the shops about January and continues until April or May. Of course, the supply does not stop during the year but as the season goes on, the animals become larger and more mature. Because of modern storage facilities and also the present day preference for the milder tasting flesh of lamb, little mutton is sold in this country and the supply is very localized.

Cooking and serving lamb

All weights are approximate. *HP* Home produced *NZ* New Zealand.

Regional names for cuts are listed after the most common name.

Lamb

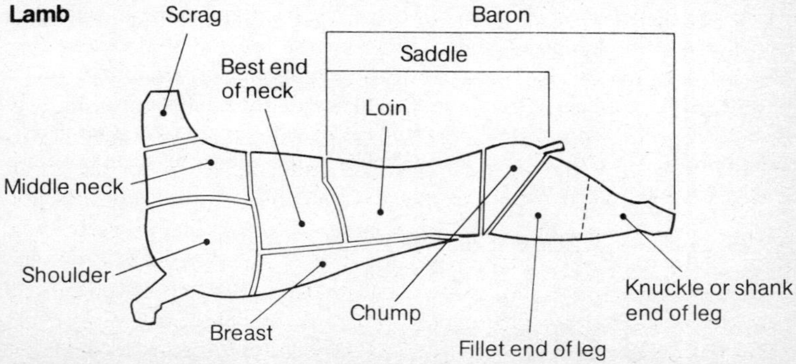

LEG, Gigot. *Roast, braise, boil.*	Prime quality meat, very lean. Lamb can be boiled, but it is usually mutton which is cooked this way and served with caper sauce. Can be cut into two, knuckle or shank end and fillet end. Weight: Whole leg. *HP* 2.25–3 kg/5–7 lb *NZ* 2–2.25 kg/4½–5 lb
CHUMP, Gigot or Leg chops. *Grill, fry.*	Only 3 chops cut from each side. Very lean with excellent flavour. Bony end piece, called chump end, usually used for stewing. Weight: Chop. *HP* 225–275 g/8–10 oz *NZ* 175–225 g/6–8 oz
LOIN, Double loin, Middle loin. *Whole: Roast. Chops: Fry, grill.*	Prime quality meat. Joints can be cooked on the bone, or boned and stuffed. It is much easier to prepare if chined first. Weight: Whole Loin. *HP* 1.75–2.25 kg/4–5 lb *NZ* 1.5–1.75 kg/3–4 lb Chop. *HP* 100–175 g/4–6 oz *NZ* 75–100 g/3–4 oz
SADDLE. *Roast, braise.*	The saddle is both the loins and chumps including the tail, cut in one piece. This joint is excellent to serve for a dinner party, serving 8–12. Weight: *HP* 3.5–4.5 kg/8–10 lb *NZ* 2.75–3 kg/6–7 lb
BARON.	This is a very large joint indeed made up of the saddle and both legs.
BEST END NECK, Rack, Single loin, Fine end loin. *Whole: Roast. Cutlets and Noisettes: Grill, fry, casserole.*	Very sweet meat. Can be left on the bone, boned and rolled, sometimes stuffed. Used for guard of honour and crown roast, chined beforehand. Also cut into cutlets and noisettes. Weight: Whole best end. *HP* 1–1.25 kg/2–2½ lb *NZ* 500–750 g/1¼–1¾ lb Cutlets (allow 2 per person) *HP* 150 g/5 oz *NZ* 100 g/4 oz

SHOULDER, Blade. *Roast, braise.*	Very sweet meat. Sometimes rather fat. Bone and stuff, and the excess fat can then be removed. Often cut into two – Blade bone and knuckle ends. Weight: Whole shoulder. *HP* 1.75–2.75 kg/4–6 lb *NZ* 1.5–1.75 kg/3½–4 lb
BREAST, Flank, Lap. *Slow roast, pot roast, stew.*	Can be fatty. Needs long slow cooking. Often boned, stuffed and rolled. If stewed, best cooked the day before, then cooled and refrigerated so that the fat sets and can easily be removed. Weight: *HP* 450–750 g/1–1½ lb *NZ* 450 g/1 lb
MIDDLE NECK AND SCRAG. *Stew, soups.*	Inexpensive cut with an excellent flavour. Allow 350 g/12 oz per person as rather bony.
FILLET. *Stew, sauté, kebabs.*	The 'eye' of the meat cut from the middle neck.
FREEZER SPACE REQUIRED	For a whole lamb, jointed. Approximate weight 15 kg/35 lb – allow 42 litres/1½ cubic ft.

Beef

These days good quality beef cuts can vary in colour from bright to dark red. One factor which will alter the colour is hanging or ageing. The butcher should hang beef for 10–14 days in a cold store. Although the flesh does not change colour while it is hanging, once it is cut, meat which has been well hung will darken. The flesh of beef which has not been hung for a sufficient time will stay a bright red much longer.

Of course, hanging large carcasses takes up a lot of space in a cold store. To make storage more economical and encourage butchers to age the meat sufficiently, some suppliers are cutting the meat off the carcass and sealing it in vacuum packs. These are carefully stored in a cold temperature. If given the right conditions, the meat will age in the packets in the same way as on a whole carcass. While the meat is in the packets, it is a dull purple red but once it has been exposed to the air for 20–30 minutes, the colour of the flesh becomes much brighter. It is often possible to buy whole cuts in the vacuum packs for the freezer and they can be excellent value for money. This beef should not be refused because of the initial dark colour.

Beef

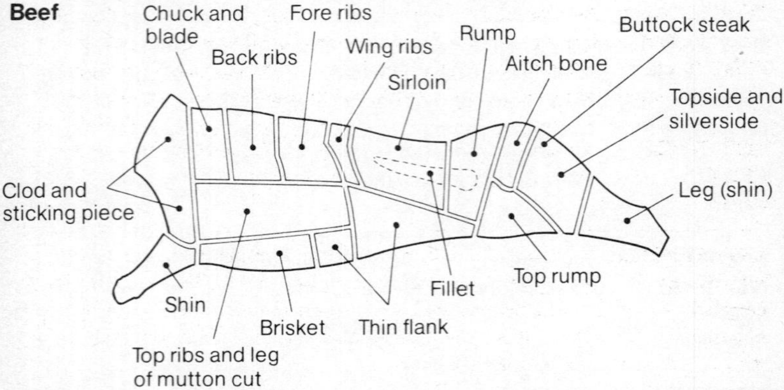

The colour of the fat is determined by the breed of the animal and how it was fed. Preference for white or yellow fat varies in different parts of the country. The amount of fat on a joint is one of personal choice, but generally these days lean meat is preferred. However, a certain amount is necessary to keep a joint moist during roasting; this is why the butcher wraps extra fat around the outside of lean joints such as topside, silverside or top rump. Far more important is that the flesh should contain flecks of fat which are called 'marbling', as these dissolve during cooking, keeping the meat succulent.

Cooking and serving beef

HINDQUARTER	
SHIN, Leg, Hough. *Stew.*	Needs long slow moist cooking to soften the gelatinous sinews. Good for steak and kidney pudding.
TOPSIDE, Insteak, Top half round. *Roast, braise.*	A lean joint, wrapped in fat by the butcher to keep it moist during cooking. Remove the fat for braising. Thin slices are ideal for beef olives.

SILVERSIDE, Soft end of bed piece. *Boil, slow roast, braise.*	Lean open grained meat also wrapped in fat. Pickled in brine, it is used for boiled beef and carrots, a traditional favourite. Horseradish sauce goes well with boiled unsalted silverside.
TOP RUMP. Round, Bed, Thick flank. *Slow roast, braise.*	Not so tender as previous two cuts but excellent flavour. For an easy family meal, pot roast it surrounded by a selection of root vegetables. For more special occasions, remove the outside fat and braise the beef in red wine.
BUTTOCK STEAK. *Stew.*	An excellent quality stewing steak cut from the top thick part of topside, top rump and silverside.
AITCHBONE, Napoleon, Tagend. *Slow roast, braise.*	A coarse grained meat with an excellent flavour. It is a large joint containing the pelvic (aitch) bone which makes it difficult to carve, so it is best boned before cooking. Weight: on the bone 4.5–5.5 kg/10–12 lb; off the bone 2.25–2.75 kg/5–6 lb.
RUMP, Popes eye, Hip bone, Pin bone. *Grill, fry.*	Cut into first quality steaks. Grilled they are delicious served with beurre mâitre d'hôtel or béarnaise sauce. Make into a carpet bag steak by cutting a slit in a thick piece and stuffing it with oysters – canned smoked ones are cheaper and add a very good flavour.
SIRLOIN AND WING RIB. *Joints: Roast. Steaks: Grill, fry.*	Best quality roasting joints. Cook on the bone, or bone and roll. Fillet is often removed, particularly from boned joints, to make them less expensive. Can be cut into sirloin, entrecôte and 'T' bone steaks. The three rib bones at the end of the sirloin are called the wing ribs. There is no fillet under them. Sirloin and wing rib are much easier to carve if they have been chined.
FILLET, Undercut. *Grill, fry, roast.*	Best quality very tender meat, lies just under the sirloin. Roasted whole, cooked in pastry or cut into châteaubriand, tournedos, fillet and minute steaks. Tail end often used for flambé dishes, e.g. boeuf stroganoff.
THIN FLANK. *Stew.*	Coarse grained meat, rather fat. Can be stewed slowly, but usually made into mince.

FOREQUARTER

FORERIB, Ribs, Rib roast, Chine. *Roast.*	Good quality meat. Cook on the bone, or bone and roll. Excellent value for money especially when a large joint is required.
BACK RIBS, Mid ribs. *Braise, pot roast.*	Medium quality joints. Good value for money if cooked by a moist method.
TOP RIBS, Thin ribs, Thick ribs. *Braise, stew.*	Medium quality joints needing slow moist cooking. Sometimes sold as leg of mutton cut – a good quality stewing steak.
CHUCK, Blade, Shoulder. *Stew.*	Good quality stewing meat, ideal for casseroles, goulash, boeuf à la bourguignonne, steak and kidney pie etc.
CLOD AND STICKING, Neck, Gullet, Vein, Sloat. *Stew.*	Rather tough. Needs long, slow, moist cooking and produces excellent gravy. More usually minced.
SHIN, Hough. *Stew.*	Needs long, slow, moist cooking to soften the gelatinous sinews. Very good for steak and kidney pudding and other similar meat dishes.
BRISKET, Point end, Horseshoe, Bosum end, Heartspoon etc. *Pot roast, boil.*	Coarse grained meat, usually boned and rolled. Excellent flavour. Needs slow moist cooking. Can be pickled in brine and boiled. Very suitable for spiced beef. The meat is steeped in spices and left in a refrigerator for 7–8 days, then boiled and pressed. Eat cold with salad. It makes a popular dish for a buffet party.
FREEZER SPACE REQUIRED	For a hindquarter, jointed. Approximate weight 66.5 kg/150 lb – allow 140 litres/5 cubic ft. For a forequarter, jointed. Approximate weight 62 kg/140 lb – allow 126 litres/4½ cubic ft.

Pork

Look for pale pink flesh with a fine grain and a little white fat. Ask your butcher to score the rind of a joint for roasting.

Pork

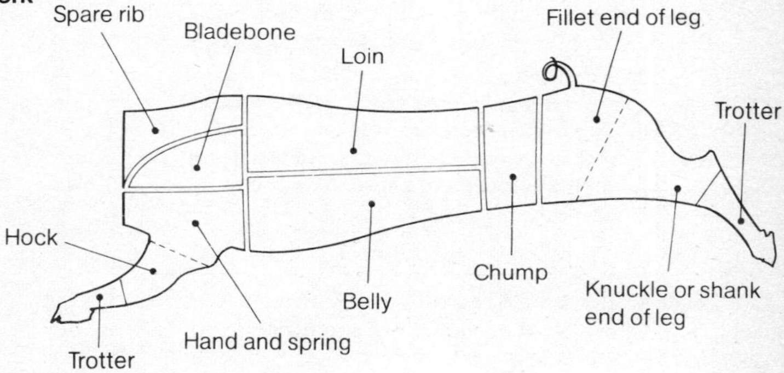

Cooking and serving pork

LEG, Gigot. *Roast, boil.*	Very lean, prime quality pork. Usually cut into two or three joints, or escalopes. Can be boned. Weight: Whole leg 5.5–6.5 kg/12–14 lb
CHUMP. *Roast, braise.* *Chops: Grill, fry.*	Prime quality meat which is better boned. Chops are large and lean. Weight: Whole chump 1–1.5 kg/2–3 lb
LOIN. *Joints: Roast.* *Chops: Grill, fry, sauté.*	Prime quality meat with excellent crackling. Can be boned and made into a very neat roll for spit roasting. Also cut into chops. Buy the weight you require. Weight: Whole loin 6.5–9 kg/14–20 lb
BELLY, Streaky. *Boil, roast.* *Slices: Grill, fry.*	Thick end of belly (sometimes called the slipper), very lean and sweet – excellent value for money. Thin end layered with fat. Can be pickled and boiled. Weight: Thick end of belly 1.5–1.75 kg/3–4 lb Whole belly 3.5–4 kg/8–9 lb
SHOULDER. *Roast, braise, stew.*	Good value for money. The whole shoulder can be boned, rolled and cut into small joints. It can also be divided into the blade bone, spare rib and hand and spring cuts.

BLADE BONE. *Roast, braise, stew.*	Very lean compact joint. Weight: 1–1.5 kg/2–3 lb
SPARE RIB. *Joints: Roast. Cutlets: Grill, stew.*	The top part of the shoulder. A long joint partially covered with crackling. Can be cut into cutlets. Weight: Whole spare rib 1.75–2.25 kg/4–5 lb
HAND AND SPRING. *Slow roast, braise, stew, boil.*	Slightly coarse grained meat, usually lean. Can be pickled. Good for stews, particularly goulash flavoured with tomatoes and paprika, or one of the substantial German casseroles with sauerkraut. Weight: 2.25 kg/5 lb
HOCK, Shank, Hough, Knuckle. *Boil, stew.*	Best cooked by slow moist method. Can be pickled in brine or boiled. Serve hot with pease pudding or cold with salad. Weight: 750 g–1 kg/1½–2 lb
FILLET, Tenderloin. *Roast, fry, sauté.*	The undercut of the loin, usually cut from bacon pigs. Very tender. Has little fat, so if roasted must be barded to keep it moist. Weight: 450–750 g/1–1½ lb
TROTTERS, Foot. *Stew, boil.*	Excellent for enriching casseroles and braises, or in making jellied stock. Can be simmered until tender and served with a sauce or finished by grilling.
HEAD. *Boil.*	Usually used to make brawn. Also cooked and added to some continental casseroles. Weight: Half a head about 2.25 kg/5 lb
FREEZER SPACE REQUIRED	For side of pork, jointed. Approximate weight 22 kg/50 lb – allow 56 litres/2 cu ft.

Veal

The best quality veal is milk fed. This is either home produced or imported from Holland. The flesh of milk fed veal is a paler pink, and more delicate in texture and flavour than barley fed veal. There should be little or no bubbly tissue, the cut surfaces should look moist and the fat should be firm and pinkish white. Choose veal with a good proportion of flesh to bone. Very small veal will come from immature animals and will have little flavour. A side of veal weighs from 17–90 kg/ 40–200 lb so buy joints of the weight you need.

Cooking and serving veal

KNUCKLE. *Stew.*	The knuckle (with meat attached) can be cut into pieces to make the well known Italian dish called osso bucco.
LEG. *Roast, braise.*	Small legs of veal cut into joints. Can be boned before cooking. Needs barding and larding if roasted.
ESCALOPES. *Fry, sauté.*	Thin slices cut from the leg.
CHUMP. *Roast, braise.*	Large chump bone makes it difficult to carve, so best boned. Needs barding and larding if roasted.
LOIN. *Joints: Roast.* *Chops: Fry.*	Can be roasted on the bone or boned and rolled, sometimes stuffed. Chops should be fried as the meat lacks sufficient fat for grilling.
SHOULDER. *Roast, braise, stew.*	Sometimes called the 'oyster'. Can be boned and rolled, and cut into small joints. Also cut up and used for stewing.
BREAST. *Stew, boil, slow roast.*	Can be cut up and stewed. Stuffed with savoury sausage meat, rolled up, tied and boiled for a galantine. Stuffed and slow roasted, but must be barded.
FREEZER SPACE REQUIRED	Because of the cost and size of veal, whole carcasses are rarely economic to buy. Approximate weight 13.5 kg/30 lb jointed meat – allow about 28 litres/1 cu ft.

Offal

Offal meats can be cooked in many ways to add variety to your meals. Often neglected but economical to buy and very nutritious, they are good protein foods. Apart from oxtail, offal has little fat. Liver is an excellent source of iron and Vitamin A and useful amounts of Vitamin D and B. Try to include liver in the diet each week.

LIVER

Choose liver which has little membrane or veining, is an even colour with no dry or discoloured patches. Allow 75–100 g/3–4 oz per person.

CALF. *Fry, grill, sauté.*	Tender, delicate flesh. Less readily available. It is generally the most expensive and is considered the finest.
LAMB. *Fry, grill, stew.*	Imported and always available. English is seasonal. Good flavour and texture, slightly coarser and darker than calf's.
PIG. *Fry, grill, pâtés*	Stronger flavour than lamb's. Excellent in pâtés, terrines, faggots etc.
OX. *Casserole.*	Very strong flavour and coarse texture. Excellent value for money when cooked slowly. Do not grill or fry.

KIDNEYS

Buy kidneys which are plump and firm, and have no discoloured or dry patches. If still wrapped in fat, it should be dry and firm. All kidneys should be soaked in cold salted water for 20–30 minutes before cooking to improve the flavour. Avoid overcooking when grilling or frying as this will toughen them.

The hard white fat around ox kidneys is the suet which can be grated and used for dumplings etc. Chop up the fat from other kidneys and render it down for dripping in the oven.

VEAL. *Fry, grill, sauté.*	Light in colour, delicate in flavour and texture. Considered the best. One kidney will serve 1–2 people.
LAMB. *Fry, grill, sauté.*	Darker than calf's and much smaller. Good flavour. For a mixed grill, allow 1 kidney per person. For kebabs or a sauté dish, allow 2–3 kidneys per person.
PIG. *Fry, grill, sauté.*	Larger than lamb's and firmer. A mustard and cream sauce goes well with the stronger flavour of these kidneys. Allow 1 kidney per person.
OX. *Pies, stews, soups.*	Dark with a strong flavour. Good for pies, puddings, soups etc. Must have slow moist cooking, cannot be grilled or fried. Allow 75–100 g/3–4 oz per person.

HEARTS

Excellent value for money. Need long, slow, moist cooking. As the meat is lean and rather dry, it is often stuffed to keep the inside moist and to add flavour. Soak well before cooking, wash under running cold water to remove any blood from the inside. Cut out the large veins.

LAMB. *Braise, pot roast.*	Smallest type, sometimes fat on the outside. Home produced is best. To add moisture and flavour, fill the hearts with a savoury mixture. Allow 1 heart per person.
PIG. *Braise, pot roast.*	Larger than lamb's. Can also be stuffed. A mixture of fried onions and mushrooms is tasty, or a sage and onion stuffing. One heart will serve 1–2 people.
CALF. *Braise, pot roast.*	Lean with good flavour, larger than lamb's or pig's. Slice and braise in a tomato flavoured sauce, or stuff with a minced pork or sausage meat stuffing and pot roast with root vegetables. One heart will serve 2 people.
OX. *Stew.*	Large and tough, produces excellent gravy. Needs long slow cooking to tenderize. Cook in a rich brown gravy with plenty of onions. A whole heart weighs about 1.75 kg/4 lb. Allow 75–100 g/3–4 oz heart per person.

SWEETBREADS

Sweetbreads should be moist and fresh looking. They are delicate in flavour and easily digested. Before cooking, soak in water for several hours until they are quite free of blood (change the water when necessary). Place in cold water and bring to the boil for 1–2 minutes. Drain and place under cold water. Peel off any large pieces of membrane. Press large sweetbreads between plates before cooking.

CALF. *Stew, braise, fry, sauté.*	Simmer gently until tender. They can then be fried lightly in butter, or coated in egg and breadcrumbs and deep fried.
LAMB. *Stew, braise, fry, sauté.*	Much smaller than calf's. Cook in a similar manner, or stew in a cream sauce.

OXTAIL

Usually cut into sections and sold by weight. The meat and fat should look fresh with no sign of stickiness. Can be rather fat and have a large amount of bone. Excellent flavour. Best cooked the day before needed so that the fat can be removed before reheating. Home produced are best. Braise or stew slowly. Allow about 275–325 g/10–12 oz per person because oxtail has so much bone in it.

TRIPE

Tripe is about the best value-for-money meat you can buy today. It is mainly protein with little fat or carbohydrate. Easy to digest, tripe is an excellent food for young children, elderly people and invalids. There are 2 types, the smooth tripe is known as blanket, the other type is honeycomb.

In England and Wales, it is partly cooked before you buy it. In some parts of Scotland, the processing may be different, so if you are in doubt, ask your supplier as it may require longer cooking. A great English favourite is tripe and onions, stewed in milk. Blanket tripe can be simmered until tender, coated with a batter or egg and breadcrumbs, and fried. In the north of England, tripe is eaten sprinkled with vinegar. The French and Italians have their own delicious ways of serving it. Allow 75–100 g/3–4 oz per person.

TONGUES

Tongues are lean but need long slow cooking to tenderize them. Choose them well trimmed of fat and bones at the root. A piquant brown sauce goes well with tongue.

OX. *Boil, braise.*	They are the largest tongues. Soak in cold water for several hours before cooking. Choose pickled (salted) ones for pressing and eating cold, and fresh (unsalted) tongues for eating hot with a sauce. Weight: 1.5–2.75 kg/3–6 lb
CALF. *Boil, braise.*	Usually sold unsalted. Prepare in the same way as ox tongue. Weight: 275–750 g/10 oz–1½ lb

LAMB. *Boil, braise.*	Sold unsalted. Soak in salted water for about 4 hours before cooking. Simmer gently until tender, then remove the skin and serve with a parsley sauce or a rich brown sauce. Several tongues can be pressed together and eaten cold. Allow 175–225 g/6–8 oz per person.

BRAINS

Lamb's brains are most usually available. An easily digested meat. Soak in slightly salted water for several hours before cooking, changing the water frequently until the brains are free of blood. Blanch in boiling water for a few minutes, then remove the skin and membranes from the surface. Put into a clean pan with a sliced carrot, onion and a bouquet garni. Cover with water, season and simmer gently for 15–20 minutes. Drain well. Then either stew in a cream or curry sauce, or sauté in butter. Or you can coat with batter or egg and breadcrumbs, and deep fry. Allow 75–100 g/3–4 oz per person.

Bacon and ham

Bacon, ham, cold meats and sausages give us some of the tastiest and most convenient of foods. In the days before canning or refrigeration, the curing and smoking of meat was essential if meat was to be kept for more than a day or two. Nowadays it is not so necessary to preserve the meat, but we continue to enjoy the many delicacies invented.

BACON

Bacon is prepared from specially bred pork, which has been cured in brine. This flavours the meat and helps to preserve it. Bacon has always been popular and today bacon production is a big business.

CHOOSING AND BUYING

Bacon should look attractively pink, and be fresh and moist without being wet. The fat should be white. If you like a mild porky flavour, choose 'green' bacon which is unsmoked. This is easily recognized by its pale coloured rind and flesh. It has been cured in brine and matured. Smoked bacon has a darker rind and flesh, and a characteristic smoky taste. Either kind should smell fresh and not rancid.

Bacon rashers are sold in several ways. In some shops they are loose and you select the rashers you want, other shops have them wrapped in film to stop drying, and some bacon is vacuum packed for longer storage. This should be opened by the date shown and then treated as fresh bacon. Do not keep too long.

Cooked gammon is often sold ready cooked. It is sliced at the counter for the customer.

Bacon cuts

GAMMON	
Whole gammon. 7.25 kg/16 lb	This is the whole leg of bacon, which is a very large joint. Can be boiled whole. Very lean.
Gammon is divided into small cuts which are also boiled.	
Corner gammon. 1.5 kg/3½ lb	A triangular joint. Can be cut into a smaller joint by cutting off gammon slices.
Middle gammon. 3.5 kg/8 lb	Prime cut from the centre leg. May be cut into smaller joints. Gammon steaks are cut from it.
Slipper. 0.75 kg/1½ lb	Not quite so fine in texture, but very lean.
Knuckle.	Part of the leg bone with quite a lot of meat. This meat is useful for soups, pie fillings etc.
MIDDLE CUT	Usually cut into rashers which are grilled or fried.
Back rashers.	These have a good eye of meat and little fat. Short back rashers have little of the streaky end.
Streaky rashers.	Lean and fat meat alternate in long streaks. Less expensive than back.
Middle cut or 'through cut' rashers.	Back and streaky sliced in one long rasher. Can be cut in half for convenience when cooking.

FORE END The shoulder and neck of the pig. It has more fat than gammon and the meat is not quite so fine. Fore end can be cut into long meaty rashers or sold in joints.

Collar. 4 kg/9 lb	Usually cut into smaller joints; tie them in shape for boiling. Also cut into rashers.
Forehock. 3.5 kg/8 lb	Sold whole or cut into smaller joints for boiling. Needs to be boned, either by the retailer or at home.

HAM

Like gammon, this is the hind leg of the pig, but for all except Wiltshire hams, the leg is cut off the carcass before curing. It is cured by dry salting or brining then drying. Some are smoked. Flavour is altered by differences in the herbs and spices used, as well as by the differences in preparation, which produce York hams, Bradenham hams, American Virginia ham, Italian Parma ham and many others. A whole ham weighs about 4.5–7.25 kg/10–16 lb and is sold whole or sliced.

English hams need to be cooked, but those from Parma, Westphalia and Bayonne are eaten raw. These are thinly sliced and served as an hors d'oeuvre, often with a slice of melon or ripe pear. Lachschinken is cured smoked loin of pork. The ham sold sliced in the grocers, supermarket or delicatessen is ready cooked. Larger pieces and whole hams are also sold ready to use. Shoulder of pork is often treated in the same way to produce the economical so-called shoulder ham.

Delicatessen meats

COLD SLICED MEATS

There are many other types of cold meats available. Some are very inexpensive, like luncheon meat and breakfast sausage which are a good standby for sandwiches and salads. Children often enjoy the more nutritious corned beef. Haslet has a delicate herb flavour as it is made from pork, pork liver and sage. This can be cut thinly and eaten cold, or fried in thicker slices. There are various chopped ham loaves, some flavoured with red peppers or hard-boiled egg. Poultry rolls, galantine and tongue are more expensive, but particularly good for salads. An attractive platter of assorted meats can make a quick meal or dish on a buffet table, that is speedily and simply prepared.

BRITISH SAUSAGES

Even the British 'banger' comes in more than one guise. There are pork sausages, a mixture of pork and beef, and herb flavoured ones; they may be plump or thin, large or small.

Black pudding In the past, this was traditional to Scotland and the north of England, but now it is enjoyed everywhere. It is made from pig's blood, with oatmeal or pearl barley, cubes of fat, onions, herbs and spices. The large curved rings are sold whole, in pieces, sliced, or you can get smaller factory produced ones. They are flavoured with herbs and spices. Grill or fry the slices (removing plastic skin first) and serve with bacon or apple slices. Also eaten cold.

Polony A pork and beef sausage with other meats sometimes added. Flavoured with spices, the exact choice of which varies regionally. It is smoked to give its well known taste. Serve cold.

Saveloys Made from pork, or pork and beef with some cereal. These can be bought fried in batter in the local fish and chip shop. At home, they are also steamed, simmered or served cold.

Haggis The plump oval shape of haggis is well known to every Scot, but these days it is also found south of the border. A blend of lamb's offal with onion, suet, oatmeal and seasoning, filled into a cleaned sheep pluck and boiled for about 3 hours. Prick with a darning needle to prevent splitting. Poach and serve with swede and potatoes.

CONTINENTAL SAUSAGES

Most of these are quite different in type from the British sausages. They can be sliced or spread and eaten with bread, salad or as an hors d'oeuvre. Some are boiled, fried or grilled to make substantial meals. They have much more meat than our usual sausages, so if they seem expensive at first glance, remember that this is the reason. Most of our British pork sausages only have 65 per cent meat, the rest is a cereal filler, and beef sausages can have up to 50 per cent cereal. You will see them in the shops sold as: French – saucisson, pronounced *so-si-son*. German – wurst, pronounced *vurst*. Polish – Kiełbasa pronounced *kew-basa*.

Garlic sausage, Bierwurst and Mortadella are all sausages to slice and eat cold.

Dried sausages There are many different dried sausages made from pork and beef. Lean meat and some fat is flavoured with herbs, spices and seasoning, filled into sausage casings and dried. Some are smoked. Whole or uncut, they can be kept hanging in a cool place for several weeks. Once cut, they are refrigerated but will still keep for some time. Salami, mettwurst, teewurst, cervelat and cabanos are all dried sausages.

SAUSAGES TO EAT HOT

If you have ever eaten a hot dog, you will know the flavour of a frankfurter. These and other similar sausages are cooked and lightly smoked when they are made.

Frankfurters A beef and pork or bacon mixture with a high meat content. Sizes are from tiny cocktail sausages to extra long German ones. They can be bought fresh or canned. Cook in gently simmering water or grill.

Eat hot with vegetables or in hot dogs, or cold in salads. They can also be added to soups and casseroles.

Knackwurst Knackwurst, smoked pork ring and other boiling sausages are eaten hot or cold. They are very good with an onion or mustard sauce, boiled potatoes and a vegetable in season. To heat knackwurst, drop into simmering water and leave off the heat for 10 minutes. Smoked pork ring will need 15 minutes.

Bratwurst The 90 per cent meat content of these makes the price higher than our usual pork sausage; therefore, a price comparison with fresh meat is more realistic.

They are made from pork and veal, onion and seasoning. Grill or fry until golden brown.

PATES AND TERRINES

There are a large range of commercially made pâtés and terrines which can be bought in delicatessens, supermarkets and some butchers. Some are smooth textured and others are coarse and rough cut. They can be made from meat and livers. Pork, veal, poultry and game are used, flavoured with herbs, spices, wine, brandy etc. Fresh pâtés are sold by weight.

Poultry and game.

Poultry includes chicken, turkey, duck, goose and guinea fowl which has been bred for the table. At one time, guinea fowl was classed as a game bird but is now specially bred for eating. Today, most poultry is reared by intensive farming methods which ensures a constant supply of fresh and frozen birds at a reasonable price.

Game is a word which describes birds and animals which are hunted and eaten. With the exception of rabbit and pigeons, game is protected by law during the breeding season and is only available at certain times.

Most game needs to be hung in a cool airy place before it is cooked to allow the flesh to age and become tender to eat. Birds are hung by the neck and furred game by the hind feet. How long it is hung depends on the weather conditions and on personal preference; some people like a rich gamey flavour and others prefer a milder one.

Poultry

CHICKEN

Chicken is one of the cheapest meats on the market today. It is an excellent source of protein in a very digestible form. Sizes of birds vary from a baby poussin to feed one, to a large capon which will feed eight or ten; it is also sold in joints. Frozen chickens must be completely defrosted before they are cooked. Otherwise, if they do not cook through completely they may cause food poisoning. Do remember to remove the giblets from the inside of the bird before you cook it.

Choosing a fresh chicken Look for a pliable breastbone, plump white breast with soft scales and small spurs on the legs. Older birds, suitable for boiling, have coarse scales and long spurs. Farm fresh birds are plucked but may not have been dressed for cooking; the weight will then include the neck and innards. This can be as much as 25 per cent of the total.

PETIT POUSSIN (Baby chicken). 350–450 g/$\frac{3}{4}$–1 lb Serve 1 per person.	Roast, braise or spatchcock, i.e. cut down the backbone, spread out flat, secure with skewers and grill. Serve with a lemon or devilled sauce.
BROILER or ROASTING CHICKEN. Can weigh as little as 1.25 kg/2$\frac{1}{2}$ lb. A 1.75 kg/3$\frac{1}{2}$–4 lb bird serves 3–4. A 2.75 kg/6 lb bird serves 6–7.	Roast, or joint and then casserole or fry. Larger ones are best roasted or cooked whole 'en cocotte'. For extra flavour, put a sprig of rosemary or thyme or a clove or two of garlic inside the bird before cooking. Before stuffing the bird, ease the skin away from the flesh and push a few knobs of butter under the skin, to keep the breast moist. Accompaniments to a roasted chicken are parsley and thyme stuffing, bacon rolls, chipolata sausages, game chips (potato crisps), bread sauce and a thin gravy.
CAPON. A large male bird, neutered by the use of hormones. A 2.75–3.5 kg/6–8 lb bird serves 8–10.	Roast. If boned, stuffed and then cooked, it makes an excellent party meal and will serve about twice as many. Slice it and serve cold with your favourite salad.
BOILING FOWL. Weights vary from 1–3 kg/2$\frac{1}{4}$–7 lb, serving from 2–7.	They have a stronger flavour and need long slow cooking to tenderize. Larger birds are more economical. Make into a blanquette or use for curry. Use small ones for bouchée fillings, salads and risotto.

TURKEY

At one time, turkeys were only associated with Christmas, but they are now available throughout the year. A small one can make a pleasant change for a Sunday lunch. If buying a large free-range bird, choose a hen up to 6.75 kg/15 lb as there is a greater proportion of meat to bone. Small cock birds are uneconomical but large ones are good value.

Choosing a fresh turkey Look for a plump breast and pliable breastbone. The skin should not be torn or the wings broken. Allow for a weight loss if the bird is not dressed.

Choosing a frozen turkey Intensively farmed birds are usually specially bred so that there is an ample proportion of flesh. It must be completely defrosted, and the neck and giblets removed.

For medium birds, allow 350 g/12 oz per person. For large birds, allow 225 g/8 oz per person.	Usually roast, with a chestnut or sausage meat stuffing. Small ones can be boiled. Sometimes, the breast is sold as escalopes, which are sautéed or fried. Legs are sold whole or in steaks. Best to sauté or braise.

DUCK AND GOOSE

Ducks and geese are now available all the year round. When buying fresh birds, look for bright yellow bills and feet. If the bird is not dressed, allow for about 33 per cent weight loss.

DUCKLING. Oven-ready weight 1–1.5 kg/2–3 lb. Serves 2.	Roast or braise, serve with young green peas and new potatoes. Cold roast duckling, served with an orange and tomato salad, makes an excellent dinner party dish.
DUCK. Oven-ready weight 2.25 kg/5 lb. Serves 4.	Braise in an orange sauce, or roast with sage and onion stuffing and serve with an apple sauce. To make it easier to serve, joint the duck in the kitchen.
GOOSE. Young gosling weighs about 1.75–3 kg/4–7 lb. Goose weighs 3–6.5 kg/7–14 lb. Serves 8–9.	Geese are fatty birds, so best if slow roasted. Prick the skin well and rub with salt before cooking. Place on a rack in a roasting tin, so that the underpart of the bird does not sit in the fat. If necessary, raise the oven temperature for the last 30 minutes to crisp the skin. Serve with sage and onion stuffing and an apple sauce. Goose fat gives a specially rich flavour to pâtés.

GUINEA FOWL

Now reared on poultry farms and available all the year. The flavour is somewhere between pheasant and chicken.

Weighs 750 g–1.25 kg/$1\frac{1}{2}$–$2\frac{1}{2}$ lb. Serves 3–4.	The meat has rather a dry texture, so bard well during cooking. Roast or casserole. Use in place of chicken or pheasant in recipes.

QUAIL

They are specially bred for the table and are available all the year.

Weighs 50–175 g/ 2–6 oz. Serve 1–2 per person.	These small birds are surprisingly meaty. Roast, braise them with white wine or stuff them with savoury rice. They are easy to bone.

Game

PHEASANT

These are protected game and can only be shot or sold fresh from 1st October to 1st February. Hang by the heads in a cool airy place until the tail feathers can be pulled out easily, about 7–10 days.

Serves 2–4 depending on size.	Young birds can be roasted, but as the flesh is dry it will need barding. Casserole older ones.

PARTRIDGE

There are two varieties in this country, the English or grey partridge and the red legged French one. They are in season from 1st September to 1st February and are at their best in October and November. Young birds have pliable beaks and feet. Hang for 3–4 days.

Serves 1–2 depending on size.	Plump young ones can be roasted. Braise or casserole older partridge.

GROUSE

The season starts in August and ends on 10th December. They are best from August to October. Hang for about 3 days.

Serve 1 per person or 1 between 2.	Roast young birds with fried breadcrumbs, redcurrant jelly and bread sauce. Casserole older ones.

WILD DUCK

Teal, widgeon and mallard are wild duck in season from 1st September to 31st January; in coastal regions, this can be extended to 20th February. Young birds have pliable breast bones, brittle beaks and bright coloured feet which tear easily.

Before cooking wild duck, be sure to remove the oil sac. This is easy to identify and lies just above the tail. The fishy flavour that wild duck often has can be eliminated by boiling the bird for 5–10 minutes in salted water with an orange, potato, onion or lemon in the cavity. Rinse the bird well, dry carefully and cook in the way you like it.

Teal These are the smallest of the wild ducks. They have a more delicate flavour and are not hung. Best in December.

Serve 1 per person.	Roast or grill young teal and serve with an orange salad.

Widgeon Considered the best flavoured of the wild ducks. Can be hung for a day but usually eaten fresh.

Serves 2.	Roast, grill or braise with port.

Mallard This is the largest wild duck. Can be hung for a day and is best in November and December.

Serves 2–3.	Marinating will help to tenderize and moisten. Roast, or cook in an orange and red wine sauce.

PIGEON

There is no close season for pigeons. They are available all the year but are best in August and September. A young pigeon has a pliable beak and breastbone, and a thick neck. Pink flesh and a plump breast are signs of tenderness. Hang for about 24 hours.

Serve 1 per person.	Roast if tender. Casserole, use in game pie or a terrine.

RABBIT

Both wild and domestic rabbits are available all the year. Some are imported frozen. Domestic ones are usually larger and have a more delicate flavour, similar to chicken. They can be bought whole, jointed or as meat off the bone in frozen packs. Young rabbits have thin ears, smooth fur and sharply pointed claws.

An average rabbit serves 3–4.	Roast whole with parsley and thyme stuffing, bard well. Joint and casserole or make into a pie.

HARE

There are two varieties, the English brown hare and the Scottish blue hare. The brown hare is considered to be the best. Young hares, called leverets, have soft thin ears, smooth fur and hidden claws. Look also for small sharp, white teeth. They get discoloured and yellow as the hare gets older. Hang by the hind feet, unpaunched, for 6–7 days.

Hare and leverets cannot be sold anywhere in Great Britain between 1st March and 31st July, otherwise they are generally available, but are most plentiful in January and February. In Northern Ireland, the season for hares is 12th August to 31st January.

A young hare weighs about 2.75–3 kg/6–7 lb. Serves 5–6. An older one serves 8–10. It is often possible to buy half a hare.	The saddle (lower part of the back) can be roasted and the rest used in pâtés. Jugged or cooked in a casserole with red wine. Often marinated before cooking to keep it moist. The blood is used to thicken and enrich the sauce of casseroled hare. If you want it, ask your butcher to save the blood for you.

VENISON

Venison is the meat of deer. It needs hanging to tenderize it. Hanging depends on age – average is 7–10 days. Flesh is dark and fine-grained, with little fat.

Roast the haunch and shoulder, if it is not damaged by shot. Stew or braise other joints and tough old animals, or use them in game pies and pâtés.

Fruit.

There is an abundance of fresh fruit in the shops all the year round, and much of it is home grown. Winter is the time to enjoy citrus fruit at their best. We have supplies of imported fruit all through the year too, especially in the winter time. Transport is highly organized to ensure that the produce reaches us in first class condition.

All fresh fruit offered for sale in the EEC countries must conform to the recognized grades.

Class 1 First class quality with no important defects.

Class 2 Good quality but may have minor defects in shape or colour. For apples and pears, etc., there are also specified sizes.

Class 3 The fruit that fails to reach the previous standards is put into this class. It is sent for processing or sold in a farm shop.

Fruit should be marked with the country of origin and, in some cases, the variety as well as the class. Prepacks have this on the label.

Fruits vary considerably in the length of time that they will keep. Buy in quantities that you know you can use and, if you cannot get to the shops too often, plan to use the fruit that deteriorates quickly first. Make sure that you have a supply of citrus fruit, apples and perhaps some green bananas or a hard melon which you can allow to mature in the warm kitchen, for use later in the week.

APPLES

The British climate is ideal for apple-growing. Home-grown apples are in the shops a good part of the year, now that they can be kept in cool gas storage, as well as being eaten fresh in season.

There are several different types of apples, varying in taste, texture and colour.

Tydemans Early This variety starts the season in August. A juicy, sweet scented apple rather like a Worcester.

Discovery A new apple with a red skin streaked with yellow. It is firm and juicy.

Egremont Russet The dull tawny colour of russet apples hides a most deliciously flavoured, crisp eating apple.

Crispin It is a yellowish green apple with plenty of flavour.

Laxton Superb A delicious sweet apple, related to the Cox's Orange Pippin. The skin is orangy red with yellow and green tints.

Worcester Pearmain A red apple with some pale green streaks. It is crisp, juicy and sweet.

Cox's Orange Pippin The colour varies, usually green flushed with orangy-red with some russet marks.

Imported apples include Golden Delicious and Granny Smith's.

Cooking apples The majority of these are Bramley's Seedling. These are excellent cooking apples, which keep well.

Storage Store apples in a cool place. If you buy in quantity, keep them separated in apple trays, just as you would if you grew them.

Variety	JAN	FEB	MAR	APR	MAY	JUN	JUL	AUG	SEP	OCT	NOV	DEC
Eating												
Tydemans Early								●	■			
Worcester Pearmain								□	■	●	●	□
Discovery								□	■			
Crispin	●	●	●	●	●	●					□	●
Cox's Orange P.	■	■	●	●	□				□	■	■	■
Egremont Russet	□								□	■	■	●
Laxton Superb	■	■	■	●						□	●	●
Cooking												
Grenadier							□	■	■			
Lord Derby								□	■	■	●	
Bramley's Seedling	■	■	■	■	■	●	□	□	□	■	■	■

■ = heavy supply ● = medium supply □ = light supply

PEARS

The British varieties are Conference, Comice and William.

Imported pears include the Beurre Hardy, Winter Nelis, Packham and Beurre Bosc.

Conference These are the rather long pears with a greenish brown colour; when ripe they are good for eating. Also excellent for cooking and bottling. In the shops from October to February.

Comice A dumpy plump shape, the Comice is a first class eating pear, being both sweet and juicy. Particularly available at Christmas.

William A green pear, changing to golden yellow. Be sure to enjoy these during their short autumn season. As they do not store well commercially, they are only in the shops for a limited period.

Storage All pears can be bought when hard and allowed to ripen at home. If you want to have some in hand, Conference and Comice pear (but not William) can be kept in the lower part of the refrigerator for a week or so, before bringing them out into a warm room to ripen. Once they are ripe, eat within a couple of days.

CITRUS FRUIT

Throughout the year, there are citrus fruits in the shops – lemons, orange, grapefruit and their relations. Prices vary according to the season and the supplies. Choose firm, fresh looking fruit; only the satsuma is ripe and ready to eat when it is still green tinged. This fruit is free of pips, easy to peel and has a good flavour. Clementines come next in the season around Christmas time. Other similar fruits are:

Dancy Type of seedless tangerine.

Kara Hybrid of the satsuma and mandarin.

Minneola Cross between a tangerine and a grapefruit.

Temple Another cross, this time between an orange and a tangerine.

Topaz Similar to temples.

Storage Store citrus fruits in a cool room temperature. Oranges, grapefruit and lemons keep 1–2 weeks, tangerines for 1 week.

STONE FRUIT

Apricots Golden yellow and yielding to light pressure when ripe.

Dates Fresh dates have a skin which needs to be removed; make a nick in the stalk end, using a small sharp knife, and slide the date out. The stone can easily be removed. They will keep for a few days in the refrigerator.

Lychees The prickly looking brown skin of these small fruits conceals a delicately perfumed white flesh and a large stone.

Mangoes The green skin turns to golden or red colouring when ripe. Allow them to ripen in a warm room. The bright orange coloured flesh is eaten raw, or made into a fruit fool or water ice.

Nectarines Similar to peaches but with a smooth skin. Rather more red toned in colour.

Peaches Look at the colour at the stalk end; when this changes from green to a warm yellow, the peach will be ripe.

Persimmons A fruit the size of a small orange, in appearance something like an orange coloured tomato.

They have a leathery skin with pips in the orange flesh. Flavour tends to be rather astringent.

Plums Buy when firm and keep until they are slightly yielding to light pressure and looking and smelling ripe.

Sharon fruit An orangy red, shiny skinned fruit. This has been developed from the persimmon. It is sweeter, has an edible skin and no pips. Needs to be well ripened.

MELONS

There are melons in the shops throughout the year but price and quantity alter according to the seasons of each kind.

Ogen Small melons from Israel, with a smooth, green striped skin and richly flavoured green flesh.

Galia This is a newer melon with a heavily netted skin. It is available from April to June.

Honeydew These melons are the commonest and least expensive. They are most plentiful in late summer and early autumn, and are easily recognized by the ribbed, dark green or bright yellow skin. If very firm, keep on a sunny windowsill until ready to eat.

Charentais Small Charentais melons, with a rough cream and green skin and orange flesh, come from France. Usually expensive, but with a superb flavour when ripe.

Cantalope The big Cantalope melon, with its sectioned shape, is the largest except for the dark green skinned watermelon.

Watermelon This is easily identified by its size and red flesh. Baby watermelons are sometimes on sale.

When melons are ripe, they are slightly soft and springy at the base, and the stalk tends to crack away from the fruit.

OTHER FRUIT

Grapes These are picked when fully ripe and will not develop further. Do not plan to store grapes for long and keep them in a refrigerator or cool place until they are eaten.

Pineapples Ripe when orange and still slightly green. If completely orange coloured, they can be over ripe. A leaf should pull out easily when ready to eat. Keep under ripe fruit at room temperature.

Kiwi fruit These used to be called Chinese Gooseberries. They are an oval fruit about 5 cm/2 inches long, with slightly hairy brown skin. Inside, the flesh is an attractive bright green with black specks of edible pips. Peel, slice and add to fruit salad or use to decorate a Pavlova meringue.

Storage Ripe fruit is best eaten on the day it is bought. Allow under ripe fruit to ripen at room temperature.

Soft fruit

Bilberries, blackberries, black, white and redcurrants, blueberries, loganberries, raspberries, strawberries all need to be used within a day of purchase. If they are to be kept until the next day, put in the refrigerator (this helps prevent deterioration). Choose firm, ripe, well formed fruit for eating or freezing. Gooseberries and rhubarb will keep for several days. If there is some soft fruit available, which is not over ripe but imperfect, it may be a good buy for jam making.

Fruit calendar

Look down the chart to see the choice of fruit available each month, bearing in mind that this is only a broad guide. Seasons can be delayed or brought forward by unusual climatic conditions which will affect the choice in the shops.

	JAN	FEB	MAR	APR	MAY	JUN	JUL	AUG	SEP	OCT	NOV	DEC
Apples – dessert	H/I	H/I	H/I	H/I	I	I	H/I	H/I	H/I	H/I	H/I	H/I
– cooking	H	H	H	H	H	H	H		H/I	H	H	H
Apricots	I	I*			I*	I	I	I				I*
Bananas	I	I	I	I	I	I	I	I	I	I	I	I
Bilberries							I	I				
Blackberries							H	H	H			
Blackcurrants							H	H				
Breadfruit									I*			
Cherries – sweet	I*	I*			I	H/I	H/I	H/I	I*	I*	I*	I*
– Morello								H	I			
Clementines	I	I									I	I
Cranberries	I	I*								I*	I	I
Custard apples	I*	I*							I*	I*	I*	I*
Damsons								H	H	H		
Dates – fresh	I	I	I	I	I	I	I	I	I	I	I	I
Figs						I*	I*	I	I	I	I*	I*
Gooseberries					H/I	H/I	H					
Grapefruit	I	I	I	I	I	I	I	I	I	I	I	I
Grapes	I	I	I	I	I	I	I	I	I	I	I	I
Greengages						I	H/I	H/I				

	JAN	FEB	MAR	APR	MAY	JUN	JUL	AUG	SEP	OCT	NOV	DEC
Kiwi fruit	I	I			I	I	I	I	I	I	I	I
Lemons	I	I	I	I	I	I	I	I	I	I	I	I
Limes	I	I	I	I	I	I	I	I	I	I	I	I
Loganberries							H	H				
Lychees	I	I	I*	I*							I*	I
Mandarins	I	I	I	I	I*	I*	I*	I*	I*	I	I	I
Mangoes	I*	I*	I*	I*	I*	I	I	I	I*			
Medlars										H	H	
Melons	I	I	I	I	I	I	I	I	I	I	I	I
Mulberries								H				
Nectarines	I*	I*	I*		I*	I	I	I	I			I*
Oranges – sweet	I	I	I	I	I	I	I	I	I	I	I	I
– Seville	I	I										
Ortaniques	I	I	I	I								
Passion fruit	I*	I*	I*	I*					I*	I*	I*	I*
Paw-paws				I*	I*	I*	I*		I*	I*	I*	I*
Peaches	I*	I*	I*	I*	I*	H/I	H/I	H/I	H/I	I		I*
Pears	H/I	H/I	H/I	I	I	I	I	I	I	H/I	H/I	H/I
Persimmons											I	I
Pineapples	I	I	I	I	I	I	I	I	I	I	I	I
Plums	I	I	I	I	I	H/I	H/I	H/I	H	H/I		I
Pomegranates									I	I	I	I*
Quinces										H	H	
Raspberries					I*	H/I	H	H	H			I*
Redcurrants						H	H	H				
Rhubarb	H	H	H	H	H	H						H*
Satsumas	I	I	I							I	I	I
Sharon fruit	I	I									I	I
Strawberries	I*	I*	I*	I*	H/ I*	H/I	H	H/I	H/ I*	HI*	I*	I*
Tangerines	I	I	I	I							I	I
Ugli fruit	I	I									I	I
Watermelon			I*	I*	I*	I*	I	I	I	I*		

H = Home produced I = Imported * = Times when likely to be either scarce or expensive

Vegetables.

No other food offers such an opportunity to add variety and interest to our meals as fresh vegetables, changing as they do from one season to the next. There are a surprising number of vegetables easily obtainable, both home grown and imported. There are a few other unusual exotic vegetables, such as yams and bitter melons, which are only found in speciality shops selling Indian, West Indian or African foods. There are also those like celtuce and asparagus peas that you will only be able to try if you grow them yourself, as they are not available commercially.

Seasonal changes
There are plenty of vegetables available in winter, such as home grown potatoes, carrots, swedes, beetroot, cabbage, celeriac and others. Not so good is late spring, when the winter vegetables are finished and the new season ones tend to be expensive and in smaller supply. Summer brings the many salad vegetables, along with asparagus, peas and beans. In early autumn, peppers, tomatoes, courgettes and marrows add to the selection. At all times of the year, there are imported vegetables adding to the choice available, though these tend to be more expensive. The large variety of frozen and canned vegetables available are a great boon to the cook in a hurry. Dried vegetables can play their part in giving variety; lentils, kidney beans, butter beans and the many other pulses can be made into excellent dishes. All these have a good food value, but it is fresh or frozen vegetables that we rely on to give us Vitamin C to keep skin healthy plus some Vitamin A and the minerals that are also needed for good health. Particularly good sources are green vegetables, carrots, potatoes and tomatoes. We grow 60 per cent of our vegetables in this country. The weather will affect supplies and consequently prices, but one can always expect vegetables to be at their cheapest during their main season. EEC regulations control the grading of produce. They also give information to the shopper about

the country of origin, weight or numbers of contents, and the growers name or trade mark, as well as the quality grade that it warrants. There are four classes of quality.

Class 1 First class vegetables with no real defects.
Class 2 Good quality vegetables but with some minor blemishes.
Class 3 Lower quality produce. This class can be suspended if supplies of higher quality are large enough to meet demand.
Extra Class This is kept for specially selected goods of excellent quality, which are not necessarily available in large amounts.

The vegetable chart that follows gives a guide to when vegetables are available. Actual supplies depend on so many different factors that local retailers will inevitably have some differences. Recent weather, local market garden trends, international politics, the cost of fuel for greenhouse heating all play a part in influencing the selection you see in the shops. Also, seasons will be earlier in those areas with a mild climate.

Vegetable calendar

H = Home grown I = Imported

	JAN	FEB	MAR	APR	MAY	JUN	JUL	AUG	SEP	OCT	NOV	DEC
Artichokes – globe	I	I	I	I	H/I	H/I	H/I	H/I	H/I	I	I	I
– Jerusalem	H	H	H	H							H	H
Asparagus	I	I	I	I	H/I	H/I	H/I	I	I	I	I	I
Aubergines	I	I	I	I	I	I	I	I	H/I	I	I	I
Avocados	I	I	I	I	I	I	I	I	I	I	I	I
Beans – broad				I	H/I	H/I	H					
– French	I	I	I	I	I	H/I	H/I	H/I	H/I	I	I	I
– mung	H	H	H	H	H	H	H	H	H	H	H	H
– runner							H	H	H			
Beetroot	H	H	H/I	H/I	H/I	H/I	H/I	H	H	H	H	H
Broccoli – calabrese	I	I	I	I		H	H	H	H	H/I	I	I
– purple sprouting		H	H	H								

	JAN	FEB	MAR	APR	MAY	JUN	JUL	AUG	SEP	OCT	NOV	DEC
Brussels sprouts	H/I	H	H						H	H	H	H
Brussels tops	H	H	H						H	H	H	H
Cabbage – winter varieties	H	H	H	H						H	H	H
– spring greens	H	H	H	H	H						H	H
– summer varieties						H	H	H				
– white	H/I	H/I	H/I	H/I	H/I	H/I			H/I	H/I	H/I	H/I
– red	H/I	H/I	I	I	I	I			I	I	I	H/I
Carrots	H/I	H/I	H/I	H/I	H/I	H/I	H/I	H/I	H/I	H/I	H/I	H/I
Cauliflower	H/I	H/I	H/I	H/I	H	H/I	H	H	H	H	H/I	H/I
Celeriac	H	H	H						H/I	H/I	H/I	H/I
Celery	H/I	H/I	I	I	H/I	H/I	H/I	H	H	H	H	H/I
Chicory	I	H/I	I	I	I				I	I	I	I
Chillies	I	I	I	I	I	I	I	I	I	I	I	I
Chinese leaves	I	I	I	I						H	H/I	I
Courgettes	I	I	I	I	I	I	H	H	H	I	I	I
Cucumber	I	I	H/I	H/I	H/I	H	H/I	H/I	H/I	H/I	I	I
Endive	I	I	I	I	H	H	H	H	H/I	H/I	I	I
Fennel – Florence	I	H/I	I	I		I	I	H/I	H/I	H/I	H/I	I
Kohl rabi	H	H	H	H			H	H	H/I	H/I	H	H
Kale	H	H	H	H								
Leeks	H	H	H	H				H	H	H	H	H
Lettuce – round	H/I	H/I	H/I	H/I	H/I	H/I	H/I	H/I	H/I	H/I	H/I	H/I
– iceberg	I	I	I	I	I						I	I
– Webbs						H	H	H	H	H		
– cos						H	H	H	H	H		
Mushrooms – cultivated	H	H	H	H	H	H	H	H	H	H	H	H
– field									H			
Okra	I	I	I	I	I	I	I	I	I	I	I	I
Onions	H/I	H/I	H/I	H/I	H/I	I	H/I	H/I	H/I	H/I	H/I	H/I
– pickling									H	H	H	H
– salad	I	H/I	H/I	H	H	H	H	H	H	H	I	I
– shallots						H	H					

	JAN	FEB	MAR	APR	MAY	JUN	JUL	AUG	SEP	OCT	NOV	DEC
Parsnips	H	H	H	H					H	H	H	H
Peas			I	I	I	H/I	H/I	H/I	I	I	I	
– Mange tout	I	I	I	I	I	H/I	H	H				
Peppers	I	I	I	I	I	I	H/I	H/I	H/I	I	I	I
Potatoes – new	I	I	I	I	I	H/I	H/I	H/I			I	I
– old	H	H	H	H	H				H	H	H	H
Pumpkins	I					I	I	H	H	H	H	I
Radishes	I	I	I	H/I	H/I	H/I	H/I	H/I	H/I	H/I	I	I
Salsify	I	I	I	I	I	I	H	H	H	H/I	H/I	I
– Scorzonera	H										H	H
Salad cress	H	H	H	H	H	H	H	H	H	H	H	H
Seakale	H	H	H									H
Seakale beet	H	H	H					H	H	H	H	H
Sorrel				H	H	H	H	H	H			
Spinach	I	I	H/I	H/I	H	H	H	H	H	H	H/I	I
Swede	H	H	H	H	H				H	H	H	H
Turnips	H	H	H	H/I	H/I	H/I	H	H	H	H	H	H
Tomatoes	I	I	H/I	H/I	H/I	H/I	H/I	H/I	H/I	H/I	I	I
Sweetcorn		I	I	I			I	H/I	H/I	H		
Sweet potatoes	I	I	I	I	I	I			I	I	I	I
Vegetable marrow							H	H	H	H		
Watercress	H	H	H	H	H	H	H	H	H	H	H	H

Cooking and serving vegetables

Boiling This is the most common way to cook vegetables. Place in boiling water with a little salt and cook until just tender. Drain and serve. When overcooked or kept hot for a long time, food value will be lost, so try to cook them to be ready just before the meal. Green vegetables, such as cabbage, keep their colour best if you boil a little salted water in a pan, add the prepared vegetable a handful at a time, keeping the water on the boil and cook until just tender.

Steaming Cook the vegetables in a steamer over a pan of boiling water. Sprinkle lightly with salt, as they do not touch the water.

Potatoes or another vegetable can be cooked in the pan below the steamer. The time taken to steam is usually half as long again as for boiling.

Fat steaming Melt a little fat in a thick pan, then add the prepared vegetables. Cover and cook over a gentle heat for about 10 minutes. Add a little water and continue to steam until the vegetable is tender. Some of the liquid may be served with the dish.

Braising This is a good way of cooking vegetables, such as cabbage, celery and chicory (blanch them first). Fry chopped carrot, onion and a little bacon in a little fat, put the chosen vegetable on top and add a little stock. Cook until tender, lift out the main vegetable and discard the rest. The liquid can be thickened to make a sauce to pour over.

Sauté Slice cooked vegetables, especially potatoes, and fry quickly in a little hot butter or fat in a frying pan until crisp and brown.

Frying Deep frying is another way of cooking potatoes to make chips or crisps. Some other vegetables such as parsnips are blanched first, then dipped in batter and deep fried.

Grilling A few of the softer vegetables can be brushed with oil and grilled. Tomatoes and mushrooms grill particularly well.

Baking Baked potatoes are a firm favourite. Beetroot, parsnips, aubergines and marrow can all be cooked in the oven.

The following chart is a guide to choosing the best vegetables when shopping, how to care for them at home, plus hints on preparing, cooking and serving. How long they keep depends on the freshness of the vegetables when you initially buy them.

SHOPPING	CARE AND STORAGE
ARTICHOKES - GLOBE Should be firm with fresh green leaves. Stale ones are dried and withered at the tips, but may still be alright to use if you only want the fleshy base.	Can be kept fresh with their stalks in cold water. Otherwise wrap in polythene and keep in the salad drawer of the refrigerator. The hearts can be frozen.
ARTICHOKES - JERUSALEM A knobbly root vegetable. Choose the largest, smoothest ones. They must be firm and crisp, and not at all soft.	Keep in a cool, airy place. Freeze satisfactorily.
ASPARAGUS Large, firm, plump stalks are best. The thin stalks, called sprue, are less expensive and good for soups. Allow 1 kg/2 lb for a first course for 4.	Best used fresh. Keep cool, wrapped and in the salad drawer of the refrigerator, but only for a short time. Freezes quite well.
AUBERGINES Fresh aubergines should have a smooth purple skin with no brown patches. They become wrinkled as they start to age.	Keep in a cool larder. They will keep for 2–3 days, longer if very fresh. May be sliced, blanched and frozen. Cooked dishes such as ratatouille can be frozen.
AVOCADOS Most varieties are green with a smooth skin, but the Hass avocado is dark and rough. They can be bought ripe for immediate consumption, or hard when you want them for a few days time. Ripe avocados 'give' slightly and feel a little soft all over when held in your hand.	Keep at room temperature while ripening for 3–5 days. To speed up the process, wrap them in a newspaper and keep in a closed container in a warm room. When ripe, keep in the refrigerator for up to 4 days.

PREPARATION AND COOKING TIPS	SERVING SUGGESTIONS
Twist off stalk, trim tips, cook in boiling salted water with a squeeze of lemon. Test to see if cooked by pulling off an outside leaf. Scoop out and discard whiskery 'choke' before serving.	Eat hot with hollandaise sauce. Serve cold filled with an oil and vinegar dressing, flavoured with mustard and fresh herbs. Pull off the leaves with your fingers and dip into the sauce. Eat the base with a knife and fork.
Peel and keep in water, with a spoonful of vinegar added, until ready to cook.	Slice the cooked artichokes, cover with cheese sauce and brown under the grill. Thinly slice artichokes and deep fry. Make soup with artichoke purée.
Tips are more tender than stalks, so tie in a bundle and stand upright in a pan of boiling water coming part way up the stalks. They cook evenly in the steam.	Eat with your fingers, dipping the tip and stalk into a sauce. Serve cold as a first course with mayonnaise. Serve hot with melted butter or hollandaise sauce.
The skin is left on if it is going to be stuffed. Otherwise, peeling is optional. Cut and sprinkle with salt to remove excess moisture. Leave for 20 minutes. Rinse, then cook.	Dip slices in seasoned flour and fry in oil. Fry in halves, scoop out and fill with a savoury mixture.
Cut with a stainless steel knife and remove the stone. Rub with lemon or vinegar immediately, or toss in salad dressing, to prevent discoloration. To peel, score down the skin and peel off in sections.	Make avocado dips and soups. Slice and add to a green salad. Cut in halves and fill with French dressing or prawn salad.

SHOPPING	CARE AND STORAGE
BEANS - BROAD Plump young beans which have plenty in the pod are best. Feel to see how full the pods are. About 450 g/1 lb in the pod will serve 2–3.	Keep in a cool place for up to 4–5 days unshelled. Freeze well.
BEANS - FRENCH Should be young, firm and crisp. Most are green, but there are yellow and purple varieties which are good to eat.	Store in a cool place for 3–4 days. Freeze well.
BEANS - MUNG Buy the seed and grow bean sprouts yourself in a warm place, or buy grown ready to eat. They should be plump and pale coloured.	The dry seeds keep for months in a dry closed jar. Fresh bean sprouts can be kept in cold water or in the refrigerator.
BEANS - RUNNER Choose young firm beans which are not over developed and stringy.	Store in a cool place for 3–4 days. Freeze well.
BEETROOT Sold raw or cooked. Young, new season ones are the most expensive. Should be well coloured and not too large.	Keep raw beetroot in a cool dark place. Keep cooked beetroot covered in the refrigerator for 2–3 days, longer if in vinegar. Freeze well when cooked.
BROCCOLI - CALABRESE Look for tight firm heads, not those about to flower.	Keep cool and for 1–2 days only Very firm fresh ones may keep a little longer. Freezes well.
BROCCOLI - PURPLE SPROUTING Look for freshness – it goes limp quickly. In the garden, pick from the side shoots as you require it and the plant will continue producing well.	Keep for a short time in a cool place. Can be frozen but tends to crumble.

PREPARATION AND COOKING TIPS	**SERVING SUGGESTIONS**
These are usually shelled, but if you can get very young ones (if you grow your own), they can be cooked whole in the pod.	Boil and toss in butter and lemon juice with chopped parsley or summer savory. Mix into a parsley sauce.
These are quick to prepare. Top and tail, and break into 2–3 pieces.	Boil, drain and toss in butter or serve in a tomato sauce. Salad niçoise is made with young beans, tomato and tuna.
Rinse off the seed husks. To serve hot, put in boiling water for a minute only, or add to a stir-fried dish and cook briefly.	Used in both hot and cold Chinese dishes. Excellent in raw salad. Add a spoonful or two to a chicken noodle soup.
Top and tail, string and slice thinly.	Boil, drain and toss in butter. Mix into a white sauce.
Do not cut raw beetroot – twist off the stalks before cooking. When cooking beetroot, or reheating it to make into a hot vegetable dish, add lemon juice or vinegar to keep the colour.	For salads it can be dressed with vinegar or French dressing; sometimes this is flavoured with finely chopped onion or grated horseradish. Hot, it can be coated with a cream sauce.
Does not keep its flavour well if kept hot, so cook just before serving.	As an hors d'oeuvre, serve with hollandaise sauce.
Trim off coarse stalks. Cook flower heads and leaves together in a little boiling salted water.	Drain and coat with cheese sauce, then brown under the grill. This is particularly good with fish.

SHOPPING	CARE AND STORAGE
BRUSSELS SPROUTS Tight green heads are best, with no yellowing of the leaves or frost damage. The Brussels tops make a pleasant change from cabbage.	Keep in a cool place or the bottom of the refrigerator for about 2–3 days. Freeze well.
CABBAGE Firm, fresh looking heads are best. Avoid limp and yellowing leaves. There are varieties for every season, such as January King, Savoy, Spring Greens and Primo.	Store in the bottom of the refrigerator, wrapped in polythene. Freezes well.
CABBAGE – RED Should be firm and fresh looking. Heads vary greatly in size.	Keeps for weeks in a cool place. Cooked dishes can be frozen.
CARROTS Best grade carrots are whole and firm. Broken or damaged roots can be used, but should be cheaper. Young carrots are sold in bunches or by weight. Old ones by weight only.	Keep cool. Do not leave in a closed polythene bag – punch holes in the bag if you are keeping them in the refrigerator. Freeze well.
CAULIFLOWER Look for fresh white curds. Yellowing or black marks show age, and old cauliflowers have a poor flavour.	Keep in a cool airy place for 1–2 days or 3 days in a refrigerator. Freezes well.
CELERIAC This knobbly root vegetable is best when medium size, without holes or damage.	Keep in a cool airy place. Discolours when cut surfaces exposed to air.

PREPARATION AND COOKING TIPS	SERVING SUGGESTIONS
Cut a cross through the stalk so that it cooks evenly. After cooking, drain and rinse quickly under running cold water to bring up the colour. Reheat in a little butter.	Sieve or liquidize to make a thick purée, add cream and seasoning. Make into a savoury mould and serve with tomato sauce.
To keep the colour, add chopped cabbage, a handful at a time, to a pan half filled with boiling salted water. Reboil between each addition.	Add chopped cooking apple or a few dill seeds when boiling cabbage. Stuff the whole cabbage or individual leaves. Use raw in coleslaw salad.
Keep the colour by the addition of vinegar or lemon juice. When it is to be used for salad, blanch briefly, drain and toss in lemon juice or vinegar with oil and seasoning.	Particularly good with rich meats such as pork, goose and bacon. Often casseroled with apple and onion.
Scrape young carrots, but peel old ones. If the oven is in use, save fuel by cooking carrots in a casserole with a little liquid.	Make delicious soups, cooked with onion and bacon. A purée of sieved or mashed carrot and potato is appetizing with sausages.
Add a spoonful of milk to the water to help keep a good colour. Cut across the stalk for even cooking.	In Poland, cooked cauliflower is topped with fried breadcrumbs mixed with chopped hard-boiled egg and parsley. Use raw or cooked in salads.
To prevent discolouration, put into a bowl of water with a spoonful of vinegar, lemon juice or citrus fruit skin.	Grate raw or cut into small pieces and toss in French dressing or mayonnaise. Purée cooked celeriac and potato.

SHOPPING	CARE AND STORAGE
CELERY Colours vary from white to green, or even pink. Fresh leaves and crisp stalks are a sign of quality. Avoid heads with frost and insect damage. Celery from the Fens area is earthy, but easy to scrub clean.	Keep moist. Wrap in polythene in the bottom of the refrigerator. In the larder, stand the stalks in a jug of cold water.
CHICORY Choose firm heads of white chicory. Green colouring indicates bitterness and browning is a sign of age.	Must be kept cool and in the dark. Wrapped in polythene in the bottom of the refrigerator, it will keep for about a week.
CHINESE LEAVES Also called Chinese cabbage. The pale, almost white leaves look rather like the shape of a cos lettuce. Often sold by weight.	Good value for money for winter salads as they keep well. Wrapped in the bottom of the refrigerator, they will keep fresh for 2–3 weeks.
COURGETTES Miniature marrows. Those 10–15 cm/4–6 inches long are the best size, although smaller ones can be excellent. The skin should be firm with no soft patches. Gardeners can grow a golden variety.	Keep in a cool airy place, such as a vegetable rack or in the salad drawer of the refrigerator for 3–4 days. Freeze sliced, not whole.
CUCUMBER Choose firm ones with smooth unwrinkled skin. Some are shrink wrapped. Straight cucumbers can be advantageous for slicing but others are often cheaper.	Cut the stalk end, then stand in a little cold water which should be changed daily, or keep in the salad drawer of the refrigerator wrapped in cling film. Keeps for 5–7 days.
ENDIVE The curly leaves of endive have a slightly bitter flavour, which is nevertheless pleasant. Choose fresh leaves, avoid those that are wilted.	Put in a polythene bag in the bottom of the refrigerator.

PREPARATION AND COOKING TIPS	SERVING SUGGESTIONS
Braise, boil or casserole. Use to flavour stews, soups and stock. Keep the leaves to use either fresh or dried for flavouring.	Serve a jug of celery with a cheese board. Chop into dice or julienne strips for salads. Apple, beetroot and celery in mayonnaise is good with ham.
Scoop out a cone of the thick base, which can be a little bitter. Rinse quickly, do not soak.	Use sliced or whole leaves in salads. Good with orange and grapefruit with a yogurt dressing. Braise the heads wrapped in bacon.
Slice off as needed for salad. Can be cooked like cabbage, but for a brief time.	Slice thinly and mix with celery, apple, pepper and nuts for a crunchy salad. To serve hot, it is best stir-fried.
When young and tender the skins can be left on, but when they get older the skin toughens and needs to be peeled.	Blanch, then add to a salad. Shallow fry, coated in seasoned flour or egg and breadcrumbs. Deep fry coated in egg and breadcrumbs or batter. Cut in half, blanch, stuff and bake.
To make cucumber more digestible, slice then sprinkle with salt. Allow to stand for 20 minutes, then rinse and drain.	Try mixing cucumber with yogurt, lemon juice, salt and pepper for a salad. Cook like marrow and serve in a sauce.
Wash, then drain.	Serve this crisp winter salad vegetable with a hot dressing of crisp fried bacon, poured over while it is still hot.

SHOPPING	CARE AND STORAGE
FENNEL Choose bulbs with fresh looking feathery leaves. A mark or two on the outer layer will do no harm. Should be firm and crisp.	Wrap in polythene and keep in the bottom of the refrigerator.
KOHL RABI This vegetable has an appearance and flavour reminiscent of turnips. Use when fairly small – up to the size of a tennis ball. Large ones can be tough.	Keep in a cool airy vegetable rack for up to 1 week.
KALE The crinkly leaves should be dark green and crisp. Best when young.	Keep in a cool airy place for 1–2 days only.
LEEKS Should look fresh. Size varies – small ones of finger thickness are delicious. Generally, choose small to medium size leeks as a vegetable. Buy large ones for soup making.	Keep in a cool airy place for a few days, or in a polythene bag in the lower part of the refrigerator. Can be frozen for use in soups.
LETTUCE Fresh lettuce has no sign of limpness, discoloration or sliminess. Some types have a firm heart, others like Salad Bowl have plenty of leaves, but no firm centre. Webbs Wonderful and Iceberg are crisp. Cos or Density are long leaved and dark green.	Wash, dry, then keep cool. In the refrigerator, put in a polythene bag, foil or box for 2–3 days. Without a refrigerator, keep dry and in a saucepan with the lid on. Iceberg lettuce will keep in the refrigerator for a week.
MUSHROOMS Cultivated mushrooms are sold as 'buttons' when tightly closed, 'flats' when fully open. They should be smooth and unblemished. The time for field mushrooms is early autumn.	Keep covered in the lower part of the refrigerator for 2–3 days. Store in a cool place for 1–2 days. Frozen, they can be used for cooking.

PREPARATION AND COOKING TIPS	SERVING SUGGESTIONS
Trim off the coarse stalks and remove the outer layer if necessary. Keep any feathery top leaves to use as a herb.	Slice thinly and add to a green salad or tomato salad. Cut into halves, blanch, then casserole with onion and tomato.
Peel thickly, then cook. It can be boiled or steamed.	Boil or steam in chunks, then mix with a soured cream sauce and sprinkle with dill. Can be stuffed or made into fritters.
Simmer gently.	Serve like cabbage.
Trim tops to a point, so that you get more of the tender centre. Leeks are often gritty between the layers; slit down and wash under running cold water. Tie in bundles if you want to serve them whole.	Boil or braise. Coat with a white or cheese sauce. Serve 'à la flamande' – Flemish style – with a topping of chopped hard-boiled eggs mixed with butter and parsley.
Wash in water with a tablespoon of salt or vinegar. Allow to soak for up to 10 minutes to remove insects etc., but no longer because it will lose valuable vitamins. It must be shaken dry, without bruising.	Add interest to green salads by including watercress, sliced cucumber, mustard and cress or avocado slices. Lettuce can be cooked in soups, soufflés or braised to serve as a vegetable.
Cultivated ones need not be peeled unless for a special garnish. Wipe with a damp cloth, or rinse in cold water immediately before cooking. Sometimes, stalks can be bought to use for soups and sauces.	Use both as a vegetable on its own and as a flavouring for many foods. Chopped and fried gently with onion and garlic, they make a good appetizer. Grill, stuff and bake.

SHOPPING	CARE AND STORAGE
OKRA Sometimes known as ladies fingers. Buy when small. They should be green and without any brown or soft patches.	Keep cool in the salad drawer of the refrigerator for a few days.
ONIONS Avoid those that are bruised or sprouting. Spanish onions are the large mild ones. Pickling onions are small and available in the autumn. Shallots are similar in size to pickling onions and are used for flavouring.	Keep in a vegetable rack in a cool atmosphere. They can be hung up in a cool dry place.
ONIONS, SALAD Spring onions, sold by the bunch, should look fresh and plump. Welsh onions are a perpetual small onion which can be left growing in the garden and used for its bulb and green top.	Keep in a cool vegetable rack.
PARSNIPS Should be clean and fresh looking, with no rust coloured patches and holes.	Keep in a cool, dry, well ventilated rack. Do not store in a polythene bag. May be frozen.
PEAS Enjoy these fresh during their short season. Plump young pods are best. Large ones, with a wrinkled pod, will be old and tough.	Keep cool and for 1–2 days only. Freeze well.

PREPARATION AND COOKING TIPS	SERVING SUGGESTIONS
Trim and slice or cook whole. Be careful to stir gently when cooking, so that they do not break up.	Okra is featured in the cooking of many countries – Africa, India, Indonesia, the Caribbean islands and the Southern States of the USA. It is made into soups, added to curries and cooked with other vegetables.
Preparing onions makes many people cry. To avoid this, work at arms length, instead of leaning over the onion. Learn to chop quickly, so that you do not stand over them for long.	Make white cream soup or brown like the French onion soup. Shallow fry sliced onion or dip the rings in batter and deep fry. Baked onions can be served as a vegetable. Stuff them to make a main meal dish.
Trim the root. Peel off a layer of the white onion skin and leave about 2.5–5 cm/1–2 inches of the green top. The tops can be used like chives.	Serve whole or sliced in a salad. When you make creamed potatoes, beat in a little of the snipped green tops.
Peel thinly and cut into fingers or slices. If they are old and hard, the centre core can be cut out. Boil, steam, roast and fry.	Roast like potatoes around a roast joint. Parboil, drain, then put in the tin and baste with hot fat. Cook for about 1 hour. Blanch, drain and dip in fritter batter. Deep fry.
All peas need to be shelled, except the delicately flavoured mange-tout peas which are cooked and served whole in the shell. A sprig of mint adds extra flavour.	Stir cooked peas into cooked new carrots. To cook the French way, sauté in butter for 1 minute. Stir in a little flour, stock, spring onions and shredded lettuce. Simmer until tender.

SHOPPING	CARE AND STORAGE
PEPPERS or CAPSICUMS Green, yellow and red peppers are all the same vegetable at different stages of ripeness. They should be firm with undamaged, smooth, shiny skins, free from soft patches.	Keep in the salad drawer of the refrigerator. When cut, wrap in foil or cling film. Freeze well.
POTATOES – NEW These should be firm. Size varies a lot.	Keep cool and dark. Green patches may develop on any potatoes kept in the light; these parts should not be eaten. If your vegetable rack is in the light, keep them in a brown paper bag. New potatoes do not stay firm for long.
POTATOES – OLD A number of varieties are available. King Edward, Desirée or Maris Piper are a good all round choice for a mealy potato which is satisfactory for boiling, mashing, roasting, baking and frying. 'White' potatoes tend to be better for chips than for boiling, although this varies depending on type. Look for undamaged smooth skins. Do not buy those with green, damaged or withered skin, or if sprouting.	Keep them cool and dark. If bought in quantity, time your purchase so that they are finished by the time the new potato season starts in May. Freeze duchesse potatoes piped into shape, ready to bake for a special occasion.
PUMPKINS Should be firm but ripe. As pumpkins can be very large, they are often sold in slices by weight.	Keep whole in a cool airy place. Cut pumpkin should be wrapped in polythene or foil in the salad drawer of the refrigerator.

PREPARATION AND COOKING TIPS	SERVING SUGGESTIONS
Remove the stalk and all the hot flavoured seeds. If you are going to stuff the peppers, this can be done from the stalk end so that they can be kept whole.	Use raw or lightly blanched in salads. On kebabs, add a few squares of peppers between the meats and other vegetables. Dice and use to flavour and colour meat and poultry casseroles and stews.
Never battle to scrape new potatoes. If they will not part with their skins, give them a good wash, then boil or steam them. After cooking, the skin always comes off easily. If preferred, serve in the skins. Cook with a sprig of mint.	Boil or steam, skin if wished, then toss in melted butter and chopped parsley. If you have leftover cooked potatoes, fry them in bacon fat or good dripping.
Peel thinly. Do not soak in water for a long time, as this causes loss of Vitamin C. Should there be any green parts, cut these off before cooking. Those to be deep fried must be dried on a clean teatowel. For baking, scrub thoroughly and prick the skin with a fork to prevent it bursting.	Boil, steam, bake, roast or fry. Make a casserole of potato slices, layering with onion and bacon, then cover with stock and cook in the oven. For duchesse potatoes, boil, drain and sieve. Add egg, butter and seasoning, mixing well. Put in a piping bag with a rosette nozzle and pipe on to a baking sheet. Glaze with egg and bake until golden brown.
Peel thickly and remove the seeds. Cut into chunks before cooking. Usually boiled.	The spiced pumpkin pie, favoured by Canadians and Americans, is made with a purée of cooked pumpkin with eggs and spices added. Pumpkin can be made into soups or used as a vegetable.

SHOPPING	CARE AND STORAGE
RADISHES Should be firm and fresh; avoid those with split roots or yellowing leaves. Size of bunches varies according to the season. In winter, there are also available long white radishes and round black ones.	Trim tops and roots, then keep in a bowl of iced water in the refrigerator for 4–5 days.
SALSIFY The long roots should be firm and fresh. Scorzonera is very like salsify but with a black skin.	Keep in a cool airy place. Can be frozen.
SALAD CRESS Sold growing in small boxes. Should be fresh and green.	As this is still growing, treat it as a plant. Keep in a light window sill and water fairly frequently.
SEAKALE The whitish coloured stalks of seakale should be firm and fresh.	Use when fresh. Keep in the salad drawer of the refrigerator.
SEAKALE BEET Also known as Swiss chard or leaf beet. The leaves should be dark green and fresh, and the centre stalk (rib) of the leaves white.	Wrap in polythene or foil and keep in the salad drawer of the refrigerator.
SPINACH Should look fresh, green and not wilted. It loses a lot of bulk in cooking so allow 225 g/8 oz per person.	Buy or pick the amount needed for immediate use. Spinach does not keep well for more than 1–2 days, even if stored in a polythene bag in the salad drawer of the refrigerator. Freezes well.

PREPARATION AND COOKING TIPS	SERVING SUGGESTIONS
Serve whole with a little of the stalk remaining to give a touch of green. Slice to use as a garnish.	Can be grated and stirred into a salad. Black radishes are peeled, grated and mixed with cream to use as a relish.
A vegetable that discolours if peeled and left exposed to the air, so put in acidulated water. Cook in boiling salted water.	Boil, drain and toss in butter and parsley. Coat with cheese sauce or make into fritters.
Cut off with scissors as required. Use fresh.	Use for sandwiches, as a garnish. Makes a tasty addition to a green salad.
Trim and wash. Tie in bundles like asparagus and cook until tender in boiling salted water.	Serve with a sauce such as hollandaise or with melted butter.
The leaves can be cooked whole. They resemble spinach but the flavour is milder. The stalks are sometimes cut away separately with the fibrous skin removed, and cooked as a vegetable.	The leaves are mostly plainly boiled, but can be served 'au gratin', or stuffed. The stalks (ribs) can be braised, served 'au gratin' or with sauces.
Wash thoroughly in several waters as it can be gritty. When cooked, chop well and drain to improve the texture.	Serve 'au gratin' with a cheese topping. Can be made into vegetable moulds and flans.

SHOPPING	CARE AND STORAGE
SWEDE This orange coloured root vegetable is sometimes called turnip. Avoid those with hard woody patches or insect holes.	Keep in a cool airy vegetable rack. Cut pieces can be kept wrapped in polythene in the salad drawer of the refrigerator.
TURNIPS Should be reasonably small, firm and without insect holes.	Keep in a vegetable rack in a cool place.
TOMATOES Firm, healthy looking ones are best. Some varieties have a less smooth and even shape than the conventional tomatoes, but these do have a splendid flavour. Soft tomatoes, if not actually bad, are often sold for frying and can be used in soups and casseroles.	Often best kept at room temperature, but if very ripe put in the salad drawer of the refrigerator. If you cannot shop frequently, buy some green ones and ripen them on the window sill so that you have a supply over a longer period. Frozen tomatoes can be used in cooking.
SWEETCORN Lift back the sheath of leaves to see if the corn is plump, fresh-looking and pale golden.	Best cooked as fresh as possible. Do not store. Can be frozen with good results.
VEGETABLE MARROW Should be a medium size. Choose smooth, firm and unblemished marrow.	Keep cool in the vegetable rack. If you have a lot of home grown ones, hang them in a net in a cool place where they are frost protected.
WATERCRESS Sold by the bunch. Look for a fresh green colour, no wilted leaves and freedom from water insects. Although usually dark in colour, there is a pale variety.	Rinse and pick over. Put in a jar of water in a cool place away from strong light. In the refrigerator keep sealed in an unperforated polythene bag in the salad drawer.

PREPARATION AND COOKING TIPS	SERVING SUGGESTIONS
This has a thick skin, so peel thickly like turnip. Boil, steam or add to casseroles.	Cook equal quantities of swede and potato. Mash together with a little milk and seasoning. This is good with sausages.
Peel thickly to remove the skin. Boil whole, sliced or cut in cubes.	Cook, drain and put in a cream sauce. Cook young ones whole.
To skin tomatoes, put them in a bowl and pour boiling water on to them. After a few seconds, the skin will split when pierced. Put into cold water to cool and then skin. Use a sharp serrated knife when slicing them for a salad.	Tomato sauce is made with fresh or canned tomatoes, cooked to a purée with a little bacon, onion, bouquet garni and garlic. Grill, fry or bake tomatoes. You can stuff them, too. A popular salad vegetable, often served with a dressing of 3 parts oil to 1 part wine vinegar.
Peel off the leaves and remove the silk. Cook in boiling water with a pinch of sugar added, until tender. Do not add salt until nearly cooked as this toughens the corn.	Corn on the cob is eaten with plenty of butter. Make the niblets into crisp fritters, a creamy corn soup or serve as a vegetable. Ground corn is the basis of polenta and corn bread.
Peel thickly and remove the centre core of seeds and fibres. Boil, steam or stew.	Make a casserole of marrow with diced onion and quartered tomatoes.
Use stalks as well as leaves when practicable, for instance in soups. For garnishing, pick over the watercress and arrange in bunches on the dish.	Use as a salad vegetable in green salads; it is good served with herring and mackerel. Use for soups, or for colouring and flavouring green mayonnaise.

Herbs and spices.

Cooking with herbs

The use of herbs is one of the easiest and most effective ways of giving individuality to your cooking. Learn the art of choosing flavours that complement the food, but never dominate it. Most herbs are fairly easy to grow in your garden, or even in a window box or in a flower pot on the kitchen windowsill.

Some herbs are very delicate and can be used in quantity but others, such as thyme, sage and rosemary are strong and need to be used with discretion. To get an idea of the flavour and strength of a herb, rub the leaves between your fingers to release the flavouring oils, then sniff your fingers.

Shopping

A few herbs can be bought fresh – parsley is usually in good supply. Sometimes, other herbs such as chives can be found in a shop and some supermarkets occasionally sell fresh mixed herbs for a bouquet garni. Generally, you either have to buy dried ones or grow your own. Some commercially dried herbs are prepared by drying in warmth, others are freeze dried – a process which preserves both the flavour and the colour. Buy in small quantities and keep in airtight containers, which are essential if the flavour is to be preserved.

In the garden

Some varieties are easily grown from seed, others are grown from cuttings. Some hardy herbs will last through the winter, for instance bay leaves, rosemary and thyme, but the more delicate ones need to be dried or frozen for winter use.

Plant herbs near the kitchen. Seed-grown ones are best picked regularly. Pick parsley and chervil from the outside of the plant so that new leaves develop.

Drying herbs

Pick shoots in the growing season. Tie loosely in small bundles or spread out in shallow boxes and dry indoors in a warm airy place. When brittle, store in airtight containers to keep the aromatic smell.

Freezing herbs

Herbs freeze well, keeping a good flavour and colour, although of course they become too soft to be much use for garnishing. Wash the herbs and strip the leaves from the stalks. Pack the leaves loosely in polythene, foil boxes or polythene bags. When required for use, remove the quantity needed, crumble or chop while still frozen and use immediately.

The bouquet garni

If the old English term of a 'faggot' were used to describe this bunch of herbs, there would probably be no mystery about the bouquet garni. It is simply a bunch of herbs which is used for flavouring. A bay leaf, a sprig of thyme (these may either be fresh or dried) and a couple of sprigs of parsley are all that is needed. Simply tie them in a bunch with a piece of thin cotton string. For some dishes, additional herbs, a few celery leaves or a twist of orange peel can be added for extra flavour. If you have only crushed dried herbs to use, put them in a stainless steel tea infuser. You can, of course, buy prepared bouquet garni in packets but, naturally, they are much more expensive. Any bouquet garni is removed before a dish is served.

Herb vinegars

Use these to flavour salad dressings and mayonnaise. Soak a handful of the chosen herb in a bottle of wine or cider vinegar for 2–3 weeks. Tarragon, basil and marjoram can be used.

Angelica

The thick green stalks of angelica are crystallized to use as decoration or flavouring e.g. in a sponge cake.

Choosing herbs

The chart gives ideas on how herbs can be used. Do not make the mistake of serving several dishes in one meal with all these flavours – it would be overwhelming. Choose one and serve with other less highly flavoured foods.

HERBS	SHOPPING AND GARDENING	USES IN FIRST COURSES AND SAUCES
BASIL A fairly small plant with shiny green leaves. Pick from the top to prevent flowering. *Flavour* A warm pungent fragrance. Use sparingly.	Purchase basil dried. This is really a plant from a warm climate, so to grow your own, start the seeds in warmth. Put plants outside or in the greenhouse to use from July to September. Freezes well.	Particularly good with tomato soups and sauces. The Genoese green 'pesto' is made from basil, with garlic, pinenuts, Parmesan and oil. This is used as a sauce for pasta or is added to minestrone.
BAY LEAVES Grow as a small shrub or allow to mature into a hedge or tree. The leaves are a shiny dark green. *Flavour* A gentle flavour.	The dried leaves are excellent. For the garden, you can buy a plant or grow from cuttings, and pick leaves as they are needed.	Part of the bouquet garni for soups and sauces. Add to soused herring or mackerel. Use to both flavour and garnish pâtés and terrines.
CHERVIL Looks like a dainty version of parsley, with flatter leaves. *Flavour* Slightly aniseed.	Dried leaves can be used. It grows from seed and will provide fresh young leaves in winter, if sown in late summer.	Chop and sprinkle on soups or use to flavour egg dishes. Mix with parsley and chives in tartare sauce.
CHIVES Tufts of spiky green leaves with mauve flowers. *Flavour* Mild onion.	Sometimes sold fresh. Available dried. Grow several clumps in the garden and cut frequently to encourage young leaves.	Cut with a knife or snip with scissors and sprinkle over soups. Use to garnish an egg mayonnaise or tomato dishes.
CORIANDER A tall, flat leaved herb. *Flavour* Leaves are delicately scented.	Can be bought fresh in Indian food shops, or grown from seed. The seeds are sold whole or crushed.	The seeds are an ingredient of curry powders, for which they are crushed and mixed with other spices.

FISH, MEAT, POULTRY AND GAME	VEGETABLES, EGGS AND CHEESE
Used in many provençale and Italian dishes. A dish of Italian lasagne al forno would not be complete without a flavouring of basil in the ragôut of meat between the layers of pasta and white sauce.	Add to toppings for pizzas. Good in pasta dishes, omelette fillings and vegetable dishes made with aubergines and tomatoes. Put chopped leaves in sandwiches with cheese.
Used in many casserole dishes as part of the bouquet garni. This is always removed before serving. Poached fish is flavoured with a bay leaf, added to the cooking liquor.	Used for flavouring some composite vegetables dishes and rice pilaf. An old fashioned flavouring for an egg custard, the bay leaf is infused in the warm milk to give a mild almond taste.
Good with lightly flavoured fish and shellfish. The leaves make an attractive garnish to cold poultry.	Add to the bouquet garni for cooking fresh peas 'à la Française'. Sprinkle over new potatoes. Often used in a mixture of chopped herbs for flavouring omelettes.
A herb butter flavoured with chives and lemon is delicious with grilled fish or meat. Add to fish cakes. Sprinkle over casseroles of poultry.	A favourite addition to an omelette. Make sandwiches with chopped chives and cream cheese. Sprinkle on salads. Blend with soured cream for a topping on baked potatoes.
Chop the leaves and sprinkle on food instead of parsley, or use sprigs as decoration. Seeds give a spicy flavour.	Leaves are used in fresh chutneys to accompany curries.

HERBS	SHOPPING AND GARDENING	USES IN FIRST COURSES AND SAUCES
DILL Pretty feathery green leaves and yellow umbrellas of flowers. *Flavour* Like caraway.	The leaves dry well and are known as dill weed. The seed is also used. Grown as an annual from seed. Freezes well.	It is especially tasty on potato or fish soups. Sprinkle on to herrings or smoked fish hors d'oeuvre, or Borshch – a Polish beetroot soup.
FENNEL Dark green or bronze feathery leaves. A tall plant. *Flavour* A taste of anise.	Plants can be divided and it seeds readily. Freezes well. If you buy root fennel, use the green leaf tips as a herb. The dried seed is sold for flavouring.	Use to garnish smoked mackerel pâté. It can also be sprinkled on soups, either on its own or mixed with parsley. Sprinkle on any fish hors d'oeuvre.
GARLIC The whole bulb is called a 'crown', the individual sections are cloves. *Flavour* A distinctive pungent flavour.	Buy the crowns in the greengrocers, grocers or delicatessen. Often sold in nets as it is best stored in a cool airy place. Garlic salt and powdered garlic can be purchased. In the garden, cloves are sown 5 cm/2 inches deep in March.	An essential flavour for a ratatouille. Also in most recipes for pâtés and cold meats. Aïoli is a garlic mayonnaise served with meat, fish, eggs and salads.
MARJORAM The lavender pink flowers with small dark green leaves are often seen growing wild. This wild variety is called oregano. *Flavour* Wild marjoram has the strongest flavour. Use carefully.	Dried marjoram or oregano keeps its flavour well. It is grown from plants or from seed. Dries and freezes well.	Sometimes add to a bouquet garni for soup, or chopped as a flavouring. It also adds spiciness to tomato sauces, when it can be used with basil.

FISH, MEAT, POULTRY AND GAME	VEGETABLES, EGGS AND CHEESE
Used a great deal in Scandinavian and Eastern European cooking, especially with fish, both chopped over it and as a garnish.	Seeds are used to flavour pickled gherkins. Sometimes sprinkled on to cabbage while cooking. Serve chopped leaves on hot or cold potato dishes.
Add to the bouquet garni used to flavour poached fish. Chopped, it can be added to a sauce poured over fish. Dried stalks of fennel can be put under the grid of a barbecue to mackerel.	Good with cucumber or tomato salad. Add to cheese dips. Florence fennel is the root variety which is used as a vegetable.
An important ingredient in many Continental dishes. Usually crushed but sometimes blanched and left whole. Roast pork and lamb can have garlic rubbed into cuts in the skin to enhance their flavour.	Crush and add to dressings for well flavoured salads. For a milder taste, rub a clove of garlic around the salad bowl. The American Caesar salad is garnished with a dice of bread crisply fried in garlic flavoured oil.
Many meat and poultry dishes can be flavoured with marjoram. In Greece, it is chopped and mixed with seasoning and rubbed into garlic flavoured lamb for roasting. Chop and add a teaspoon to a spicy chilli con carne.	Blends well with mushrooms and tomatoes. A popular herb in Italy, it flavours many of the dishes of pasta or polenta. Try it added to the stuffing for cooked courgettes, too. Sprinkle over pizzas before topping with cheese.

HERBS	SHOPPING AND GARDENING	USES IN FIRST COURSES AND SAUCES
MINT There are a number of varieties of mint. They all have the characteristic minty smell. *Flavour* Varies with type – spearmint reminds you of chewing gum; peppermint, of toothpaste.	Buy it dried, or preserved with vinegar in jars ready to use. Mint spreads in the garden, so limit the space it is allowed. It grows readily from root cuttings.	Chopped mint blended with vinegar and a little sugar makes the lovely fresh mint sauce to serve with lamb. Use it to flavour and garnish tomato juice cocktails. Chilled yogurt soups made with cucumber and shellfish can have mint sprinkled on top.
PARSLEY Most parsley has the familiar curly leaf, but there is also a flat leaf French parsley and Hamburg parsley, which has the root used in cooking. *Flavour* A good flavour which brings out the best in many foods.	Use dried or fresh parsley. When fresh it is sold by weight or in bunches. Can be frozen – it keeps its flavour well. Grows fairly easily, especially if started in warmth.	Sprinkle soups with chopped parsley, to add a fresh green colour. Use chopped or in sprigs to garnish hors d'oeuvre. Stir into a white sauce to serve with fish or ham.
ROSEMARY A bush closely covered with thin spiky leaves, deep green on top and silver grey underneath. Pale blue flowers. *Flavour* Strong – use with care.	Dried rosemary has a good flavour but a hard, brittle texture. As it is an evergreen shrub, a bush in the garden is a great help to the cook.	Often added to a marinade of wine, carrot, onion, peppercorn, bay leaf and thyme. This is used to soak tough meats such as stewing steak and venison, to make them tender and tasty.

FISH, MEAT, POULTRY AND GAME	VEGETABLES, EGGS AND CHEESE
Roast lamb with mint sauce is a British tradition. For a change, make an apple jelly and add chopped mint. Tabbouleh is a Lebanese salad made from soaked crushed wheat, tomatoes, onion, oil and lemon juice with plenty of chopped mint and parsley.	Put a sprig with new potatoes or peas while they are cooking. Add a little extra chopped mint when they are served, if you want to accentuate the flavour. With curry, serve a cooling side dish of plain unsweetened yogurt with cucumber and mint.
Chopped or in sprigs, it makes a tasty and attractive garnish which is rich in Vitamin C. Use stalks only in a bouquet garni and keep the tops for garnish. An important flavouring for many stuffings.	Sprinkle over vegetable or salad dishes. Use with mixed herbs for an omelette. Add to savoury croquettes and dishes made from cooked potato. Mix into cream or cottage cheese for salads; blend with salad dressings.
A sprig of rosemary is added to a bouquet garni for a coq au vin. Lamb and pork can be spiked with the finely chopped soft leaf tips of rosemary, mixed parsley and garlic; or a sprig of rosemary put in the roasting tin.	Too strong for lightly flavoured eggs. A little is added to the sauce for some pasta dishes.

HERBS	SHOPPING AND GARDENING	USES IN FIRST COURSES AND SAUCES
SAGE A low growing, woody plant with greyish green oval leaves. There are also purple and golden leaved varieties. *Flavour* A distinctive strong flavour, to be used with care.	Excellent dried. Also used in ready made packet stuffings. Grows from seed or rooted branches.	Used in some Italian dishes. Sage bread is made in the region of Liguria. A sprig is added to chicken liver recipes, such as chopped chicken livers on toast.
TARRAGON An untidy looking herb with dark green leaves on wiry upright stalks. *Flavour* An excellent flavour. Not over strong when used sensibly, rather peppery if too much is added.	Tarragon can be dried for winter, but is better frozen. The French variety has the best flavour; it is grown from rooted cuttings	The classic herb for a buttery béarnaise sauce. Tarragon sauces are served with many dishes. Chopped, it can be sprinkled over soups or on a vegetable, e.g. cucumber or tomatoes in a mixed hors d'oeuvre. Tarragon vinegar is flavoured with sprigs of the herb.
THYME A low growing plant with small leaves and lilac flowers. There are several different varieties. *Flavour* A pungent herb used frequently but in small quantities. Needs care in use.	Dried thyme has a good flavour. It grows from seed or plant – there are several varieties including lemon thyme.	A usual ingredient in a bouquet garni and as such used in many dishes.

FISH, MEAT, POULTRY AND GAME	VEGETABLES, EGGS AND CHEESE
Duck, goose and pork are excellent with sage and onion stuffing. A leaf put in a pigeon before cooking gives a good flavour. Add to sausages and pork pies.	Sage Derby cheese is flavoured with crushed sage leaves. Vegetable kebabs for your barbecue can have sage leaves put between the peppers, tomatoes and mushrooms.
Trout in a creamy tarragon sauce is splendid. Good in the bouquet garni for fish and chicken. Roast a chicken with a handful of tarragon inside instead of stuffing, then add chopped tarragon to the gravy.	Salads of many kinds can be subtly changed with this herb. Try adding it to a potato mayonnaise or a mixed salad.
Chopped in potted meats, with mixed herbs and in bouquet garni.	Chopped and then mixed into herb butters or herb cheese. The flavouring for thyme vinegar.

How to use spices

The warm fragrance of spices adds zest to good food. They have been enjoyed in this country for hundreds of years. In the days of the early spice trade they were as precious as gold. Today, saffron, vanilla and cardomom are fairly expensive but others are cheap and, therefore, spices can be used by everyone.

Spices are the roots, bark, seeds and other parts of plants. The hot countries of the tropics supply many of the spices that we use. It is important to know the kind of taste that you get from each one that you use, so you can gauge the amounts to put in your dishes, and use them with discretion and understanding.

SPICES	THEIR USES
ALLSPICE or JAMAICAN PIMENTO Whole, reddish brown berries. They look similar to black pepper, but are slightly larger. The flavour resembles a mixture of cinnamon, nutmeg and cloves.	Use either whole or ground in making chutneys and pickles; also in both sweet and savoury dishes.
ANISE SEED Buy these small liquorice flavoured seeds whole or ground. **Star anise** Star shaped seeds with a similar flavour. Crush or use whole.	Add to spiced tea breads, and other cakes and biscuits. Gives a delicate light spiciness in Chinese cookery. The flavouring for many drinks, such as Sambuca, Ouzo and Pernod.
CARAWAY SEED Small curved seeds with an aromatic smell.	Seed cake is a rich Madeira cake with caraway seeds added. They are a delicious addition to breads, particularly rye breads. Also cooked with sauerkraut and cabbage.
CARDOMOM Buy in the pods, or as shelled or ground seeds. It has a light scented taste.	Hot punches are flavoured with this spice, crushed and steeped in the wine. In the Near East, it is a flavouring for coffee as well as foods.

CASSIA Pieces of rough bark similar in flavour to cinnamon. **CINNAMON** Stick cinnamon is curled bark. Both cassia and cinnamon can be bought ground to a powder.	Many cakes, biscuits and puddings have cinnamon used as a single spice or in a mixture of spices. A teaspoonful in a chocolate cake is excellent. Stick cinnamon is put in hot punches, or can be added when stewing apples or plums.
CAYENNE A very hot red chilli pepper sold in powder form.	Do not confuse with paprika. They look similar but cayenne is very hot. A small pinch enlivens a cheese soufflé or a tomato sauce.
CELERY SEED Small seeds with a definite celery taste. **Celery salt** Crushed celery seed with salt.	Pleasant to use for flavouring soups, sauces, pickles and savoury dishes. Particularly useful when you have no fresh celery.
CHILLIS These look like long thin peppers, in colour ranging from green, to yellow and red. They are all hot, some more so than others. Use fresh or dried.	Add to curries, pilaf, chilli con carne. Wash your hands immediately you have cut chillis; on no account touch your eyes or nose after handling them, as this causes a painful stinging. To prepare chillis, cut in half and remove the seeds, then slice them. Use dried chillis whole as a flavouring and remove before serving.
CLOVES These dried flower buds are an aromatic spice which can be bought whole or ground.	Used whole, put two or three in an apple pie, or stick one in an onion when making stock. Stud the top of a baked ham with cloves. Add to pickled fruit or put in a hot wine punch.
CORIANDER Whole coriander seed has a husk which contains small seeds. Buy whole or ready ground. A light fragrant taste with a hint of lemon.	An ingredient of many curry powders, and one which is often used in homemade curries. Dishes named 'à la Grecque' contain coriander. Also a flavouring in cakes and biscuits.

CUMIN

Buy whole seeds or ground. A light aromatic spice.

An ingredient in curry powders. Used with meats, and in sausages and pickles. It gives the distinctive taste to Munster cheese from Alsace. Used in Indian and Mexican food. Pretty pale green balls of crystallized cumin can decorate cakes and puddings.

FENUGREEK

Small hard seeds or ground, with a distinctive curry flavour.

Used to flavour chutneys and curries. Add a spoonful to a beef stew or a thick vegetable soup, to give a light subtle flavour.

GINGER

Buy dried root, ground, fresh root or preserved. Fresh ginger can be peeled and stored in a freezer.

Used in Britain since Mediaeval times for gingerbread and other cakes; more recently for ginger beer, ginger ale and ginger marmalade. Used fresh in Chinese and Indian cookery.

JUNIPER BERRIES

Looks like allspice or black pepper, with a distinctive smell of gin.

Put whole berries in marinades and sauerkraut dishes. Crushed, as a spicy addition to a meat pâté, braised venison or rollmop herrings. Gin is, of course, flavoured with them.

MACE

The outer membrane of the nutmeg. The flavour is similar, though milder. Sold as blades of mace or as a powder.

Blends with both sweet and savoury foods. Add to marinades and sauces, especially bread sauce. Can be added to the biscuit crust for a cheesecake. Also used in spiced cakes.

MUSTARD

Sold powdered or ready made. Also as mustard seed. English mustard is very strong. French ones mostly milder, and are blended with wine to give a different taste.

Gives a hot spicy flavour to pickles and relishes. Use to add flavour to French dressing and mayonnaise. Serve mustard sauce with mackerel and herrings. Mostarda is an Italian relish of candied fruits in mustard flavoured syrup, from the town of Cremona.

NUTMEG	
Best used whole and grated as required. It can be bought ready ground but loses flavour rapidly.	Sprinkle a pinch over cabbage, Brussels sprouts or creamed potatoes. Grate over rice pudding or junket. Add to teabreads and spiced cakes. Sprinkle on hot egg nog.
PAPRIKA	
A red pepper prepared from dried sweet peppers from Spain and Hungary. Flavour can vary from mild to hot; but the best quality paprikas are usually mild and bright red in colour.	Hungarian goulash is coloured and flavoured with paprika, so is Liptauer cheese. Add to plain unsweetened yogurt for salad dressings; sprinkle on dressed crab, chicken salads, egg mayonnaise and other pale coloured foods.
PEPPER	
Both black and white pepper are sold whole or ground.	Flavour is best when freshly ground. Used in most savoury dishes. White pepper is useful in white sauces such as mayonnaise, cream sauces and hollandaise sauce.
Green peppercorns are sold in cans.	Crushed and put in a sauce for steak or duckling.
SAFFRON	
One of the most expensive spices. It both flavours and colours food. Buy in powder form (sometimes this is sold in thimbles) or the stamens sold in packets.	Traditional in Cornwall for making saffron cake, in Spain for paella, and in Italy for risotto. Saffron rice is made by soaking saffron in boiling water, then using this as part of the rice cooking water. Saffron is indispensable for bouillabaisse soup.
TURMERIC	
A vivid yellow powder.	Gives colour and flavour to rice, curries and mustard. Used in mustard pickles.
VANILLA	
Pods are sold, often in pairs. Some real vanilla essences are available but most are synthetic.	Custards, creamy puddings, ices, sponge cakes and a multitude of sweet dishes are vanilla flavoured. Pods are used to flavour sugar and also liquids. Steep the pod in the warm liquid (e.g. the milk for an egg custard) until flavoured. Wash the pod, dry in a warm place and keep in an air-tight jar ready to re-use. Slit the pod when you want to release more of the flavour.

Cookery

Eat well, eat wisely.

Good health depends on many factors and one of these is a good diet. Unfortunately, we do not instinctively eat the right foods for good health, so knowledge must take the place of instinct, both in our choice of foods and in the amount we eat.

BASIC EATING PLAN – FOODS TO EAT EACH DAY

Meat, fish, eggs, cheese

You need two helpings from this group daily. Vary these foods during the week. They are the body building protein foods which are needed for growth, and for repair and renewal of tissue. Pulses (dried peas, beans, lentils) add to the protein in the diet.

Milk, cheese and yogurt

Children and teenagers need calcium and phosphorus for growth of teeth and bones. The amount required daily is the equivalent to that found in 600 ml/1 pint milk or 75 g/3 oz cheese. Adults need only half this quantity. Milk is also a major source of riboflavin; this is lost when milk is left in the light on the doorstep. Yogurt has much the same food value as milk, except that it has a little less fat.

Bread and cereals

Bread and flour products contain carbohydrates for energy. They also contribute protein, minerals and vitamins. Wholemeal bread has a valuable amount of roughage, most important to the digestive system.

Vegetables and salads

These provide essential minerals, vitamins and fibre needed for the correct working of the bodily functions. Eat at least two vegetable portions each day. Vary the selection during the week as each one is nutritionally different. Potatoes are a main supplier of Vitamin C.

Fruits

Eat at least one piece of fresh fruit each day and vary these through the week. They also contain fibre. The Vitamin C present in most fruits, particularly citrus fruit, strawberries and blackcurrants, helps to keep the skin, gums and muscles healthy.

FOODS TO EAT IN MODERATION

Of all the foods that we eat, sugar is the one that is empty of all nutrients except carbohydrates. It will do no harm if you eat little or no sugar, and it is the first thing to cut if you want to slim. It is wise to keep rich, sweet puddings, cakes and confectionery for party occasions.

Avoid these foods if overweight, and eat in moderation:

Fried foods, cream and butter sauces, oily salad dressings, biscuits, cream, chocolates, sweet drinks and alcohol.

DAILY EATING GUIDE

BREAKFAST Many people find that they feel more alert and able to work better when they have started the day with breakfast, and many think that children work better at school when they have had one, too. For a light breakfast, cereal with milk, bread and butter or toast, tea or coffee, or for a more substantial one, bacon and eggs, or a savoury egg dish, baked beans or cheese on toast, or kippers or fishcakes. Grapefruit or fruit juice would be a good addition to either type of breakfast.

MAIN MEAL This may be eaten at midday or in the evening. A main meal should include a body building protein food (meat, poultry, offal, fish, eggs or cheese) and vegetables or a salad. Starchy foods are included, such as potatoes and bread. These add some important vitamins and minerals, but should be used in moderation. If you serve a main dish with pastry, choose a light pudding or fresh fruit.

Main meal choice. Select a meat, fish, egg, cheese or vegetarian dish:

Meat dishes – Roasts, grills, casseroles, mince, sausages, steak and kidney pudding or pie, kebabs, made up dishes, curries, cold sliced meats with salad. Textured vegetable protein (TVP) can be used to extend some of these when cost is important. Offal is particularly good food value, liver and kidneys are rich in iron (needed to prevent anaemia) and vitamins. Serve liver or kidneys every 7–10 days.

Fish – Poached, grilled, baked, made into fish pies or risotto. Fried fish occasionally. Fish with salad, e.g. sardines, pilchard, tuna, smoked mackerel, fish pâté.
Eggs – Omelettes, soufflés (often with cheese or ham to flavour) quiche Lorraine and other savoury dishes, hard-boiled eggs with mixed salad, pancakes.
Cheese – Salads, soufflés, flans etc.
Vegetarian – Dishes made with pulses, nuts or TVP.

VEGETABLES OR SALAD Serve vegetables or a salad with any of main meal dishes. Two vegetables of different kinds ensures a variety of nutrients; one usually being potato which is rich in Vitamin C. Green vegetables and carrots especially should be served regularly. Take care not to overcook vegetables, as this destroys the Vitamin C. Ideas will be found in the vegetable section of this book.

PUDDINGS Fresh fruit rather than a cooked pudding is a good choice, especially if it is not included in other meals in the day. The Vitamin C in fresh fruit is needed each day, as this vitamin cannot be stored in the body. Milk puddings are an easy way to incorporate milk, especially for the very young and the elderly. Make custards, rice puddings, semolina, blancmange or milk jellies. Puddings with a limited amount of sugar, starch and cream are best for everyday eating, keep the rich creamy puddings for special occasions. Fruit pie or other recipes using pastry should only be given when there is no pastry in the main course. Cheese and buscuits are a high protein alternative to a pudding.

AGE MAKES A DIFFERENCE

At each stage of life we have different needs, and it is vital to the health of each member of the family to be aware of these. Babies, children, teenagers, adults and older people each have their own requirements.

Babies The ideal food for babies is their mother's milk; all the necessary nutrients are there, ready, and at the right temperature. It also helps to give natural protection against disease, is hygienically clean and there is no danger of it causing allergies.

Baby milks have been modified to make them as near to mother's milk as possible. Great care must be taken when making up the feeds to ensure they are the correct strength. Orange juice, rosehip syrup or blackcurrant juice are given from an early age to provide Vitamin C. When solid foods are introduced, egg yolk is included so that some iron is given (a newborn baby has only enough iron to last it over the first few months of life). When vitamin supplements are prescribed, make sure they are measured properly.

Later, the baby is gradually weaned on to a mixed diet and advice should be sought as to the foods to give at this time. Milk continues to be a very important food (and also cheese and yogurt), as the calcium in milk is necessary for growth of bones and teeth. Vitamin D must also be present to aid this important development. Protein foods are needed for growth, too.

The pre-school child Between one and five years old, children grow rapidly. They are also forming their eating habits, therefore meal times should be quiet, regular and relaxed. Meals should include meat, fish, eggs, cheese, beans, bread and other cereals, which are all foods for growth and energy. About 600 ml/1 pint milk each day gives all the calcium a child needs as well as other minerals and vitamins. If a child does not drink milk regularly, include in other dishes.

The school child and teenager The right foods are vital all through the time of growth, and young people particularly need calcium, phosphorus and Vitamin D for sturdy bones and teeth. Calcium is obtained from milk, cheese, yogurt, white bread and flour, green vegetables, canned fish and tripe. Phosphorus is found in many foods, so it is never likely to be short.

Vitamin D is in margarine, fatty fish, eggs, butter and cheese. It is also made in the body by the action of sunlight on the skin.

Teenage girls, like adult women, need to have sufficient iron-rich foods. Meat, especially liver, heart, kidneys and corned beef, bread and flour, green vegetables, eggs, baked beans, dried apricots and other dried fruit and cocoa powder are all good sources of iron. Iron from animal sources is best. Vitamin C from fruit and vegetables must be included in the daily diet to aid the absorption of the iron.

Adult men Men need a nourishing diet if they are to keep healthy. The amounts of food required depend on the level of activity – a man in an office job, who is sitting down for much of the time, will need less than a man doing heavy physical work. Protein is still needed by all adults to replace tissue; most people in this country eat more than enough for their requirements.

Adult women Like men, women also must have an adequate intake of the right foods, especially sufficient iron otherwise they may become anaemic. Care should be taken to avoid sweet snacks.

During pregnancy and breastfeeding, food assumes even greater importance, since both the mother and her developing baby are dependent on the type of food she eats. It is essential to have sufficient of the bone forming foods as already described for young children. More protein is also needed as well as iron and vitamins. Milk and cheese are important foods at this time as part of a good mixed diet which includes fish, meat, eggs, vegetables and fruit. Vitamin and iron supplements may be prescribed.

Older people They also require a balanced diet, though their energy requirement has become less. Protein foods, vegetables and fruit are still important, with some carbohydrates (bread, flour and fats products). Calcium, phosphorus and Vitamin D are still necessary to prevent bones from becoming brittle. About 300 ml/½ pint milk a day is recommended.

DIETARY DANGERS

Overweight Many children and adults are overweight in this country. This condition is caused by constantly eating more than is necessary. Every time you take in more energy in the form of food or drink than you expend in activity, this surplus is converted into fat. The unnecessary extra foods tend to be the carbohydrate foods (sugar, alcohol and starch) and fat, so these are the ones to cut out when you want to lose weight. Cakes, biscuits, jam, sugar, sweets, puddings and alcoholic drinks can all be omitted from your meals and snacks if you want to lose extra inches. Some bread and potatoes are included in many slimming diets; this is because they supply valuable amounts of vital nutrients.

Teeth Vitamin C is needed for healthy gums, and calcium and Vitamin D are needed for strong teeth. Decay of teeth is caused by sweet sticky foods left on the teeth, and these cause damage to the tooth enamel. The habit of cleaning teeth after meals is one that should be encouraged. Children should be taught to eat an apple, piece of carrot or cheese, if they cannot clean their teeth on occasions. Allow children one or two sweets at a specific time, so that they are not constantly wanting and nibbling sweets.

Nutrients and their sources

WHICH FOODS TO EAT	WHY WE NEED THEM
PROTEINS	
Lean meat, fish, eggs, cheese, milk are the animal proteins. Those from vegetable sources include nuts, seeds, pulses and cereals, these are not complete proteins.	Necessary for growth in children, and repair and renewal of tissue in adults. Plan food so that an adequate amount of carbohydrates and fats are included to give energy, then the protein foods can fulfil the functions of growth and repair.
FATS	
Butter, margarine, cheese, vegetable oils, cream, lard, dripping, fatty meat and fish, nuts, fish liver oils.	Small amount of fat is needed for normal health. Fat makes some foods more palatable. Vitamins A and D are fat soluble and are found in most of these foods.
CARBOHYDRATES	
Sugar, rice, pasta, jams, honey, dried fruits, cakes and pastries, sweets, puddings, bread, potatoes, root vegetables.	Produce heat and energy. More is needed by very active people than by those living sedentary lives.
MINERALS	
Calcium	
Milk, cheese, yogurt, watercress, green vegetables, tripe, figs, almonds, canned fish e.g. sardines, salmon (with soft bones that can be eaten), white flour, bread.	Essential for growth and maintenance of bones and teeth. Also required for blood clotting and muscle functions. Vitamin D must be present for absorption of calcium.
Iron	
Meat, offal, corned beef, eggs, cocoa, chocolate, apricots and other dried fruit, wholemeal and white flour, bread, green vegetables, potatoes. (Vitamin C must be in the diet too, if the iron is to be absorbed as well as possible.)	Forms part of the red pigment of the blood which carries oxygen around the body. Also present in muscles. Particularly important for teenage girls and women. Shortage causes anaemia, which needs medical rather than dietary cure.

Note There are a number of other minerals needed in small amounts. These are not likely to be in short supply in a good varied diet.

WHICH FOODS TO EAT	WHY WE NEED THEM
VITAMINS These special substances, essential for good health, are needed regularly by the body. Each vitamin is found in particular foods.	
Vitamin A Butter, margarine, liver, kidney, milk, fish liver oils (from cod and halibut). Dark green vegetables such as spinach and watercress; yellow vegetables such as tomatoes and carrots. Also cheese, eggs and dried apricots.	For seeing in a dim light; for the health of skin and moist surface tissues. Excess dosages of cod or halibut liver oils are poisonous.
Vitamin B This was first thought to be a single substance, but later proved to be almost a dozen different ones. These will all dissolve in water, so do not use too much water for cooking vegetables and, where suitable, use the water to add to gravy, soups etc. When you cook meat, the juices also contain B vitamins, so include when making gravy.	
Thiamin Vitamin B1 Bread, flour, meat, potatoes, milk, oatmeal, fortified breakfast cereals, Marmite. **Riboflavin** Vitamin B2 Milk, meat, liver, eggs, cheese, kidney, Marmite, green vegetables. This vitamin is destroyed by sunlight, for example, if milk is left on the doorstep unprotected from the sun. **Niacin** Meat and meat products, fish, bread, flour, bran, brown rice, fortified breakfast cereals, milk, meat extract, Marmite, vegetables. It is widely distributed in many other foods as well. **Other B vitamins** Meat, fish, eggs, some vegetables including raw green leafy vegetables, pulses.	The B vitamins held to keep the nervous system and blood healthy. They are needed in order to release energy from starch and sugar foods and allow full use of the protein we eat.

WHICH FOODS TO EAT	WHY WE NEED THEM

Vitamin C

Fresh vegetables and fruit, in good condition, provide Vitamin C. It dissolves in water so do not soak foods for long, and cook them in the minimum amount of boiling water. Heat also destroys it, so cook foods for the shortest time necessary. A lid on the pan helps to reduce the loss. The addition of bicarbonate of soda destroys the vitamin. Do not keep vegetables hot for long after cooking. It is lost when vegetables are dehydrated. If you use dried potato, make sure that you buy one with added Vitamin C.

Fresh vegetables and fruit, including correctly frozen ones. Canned vegetables lose about half their Vitamin C in processing, but this is a little less than the loss in normal cooking. Therefore, heat canned vegetables for the minimum time and eat straight away. Raw fruit such as blackcurrants, strawberries, citrus fruits, pineapple. Green vegetables, tomatoes, potatoes.	Although most nutrients are stored in our bodies for a time, Vitamin C is not stored. Therefore, we need to have some fruit and vegetable every day. It is necessary for healthy skin and the connective tissues of the body. Shortage of this vitamin means that wounds heal more slowly, and the health of gums may be affected.

Vitamin D

This is the only vitamin made in our bodies by the action of sunlight on the skin. Almost all the Vitamin D needed can be made in this way. However, some people get little sunlight, particularly housebound invalids and elderly people who rarely go out. They especially need Vitamin D in their diet.

Margarine has Vitamins A and D added during manufacture. Butter (variable amounts), oily fish e.g. sardines, herring, kippers, and eggs, evaporated or dried milk with added Vitamin D.	Calcium and phosphorus must be in the diet with Vitamin D. This is absolutely essential for the growth and strength of bones and teeth, so it is especially vital during the growing years, pregnancy and breastfeeding. Where there is a grave insufficiency, a child can develop rickets – a bone disease. Elderly people can develop brittle bones if their diet is short of Vitamin D and calcium. Cod liver oil, halibut oil and vitamin preparations can be used to supplement the diet. Taking the correct dose is vital.

WHICH FOODS TO EAT	WHY WE NEED THEM
Vitamin E Vegetable oils, cereal products, eggs.	In most foods. The exact need is not yet fully established.
Vitamin K Fresh dark green vegetables such as kale, spinach, cabbage. Cauliflower, peas, cereals.	Necessary for blood clotting. As it is made in the body as well as being obtained from a wide variety of foods, Vitamin K is rarely short.

Planning meals

When planning and preparing meals, good flavour and appearance are important, and the right selection of food is vital for nutritional value.

Budgeting
It makes sense to plan your meals, allowing a certain amount of money for food and making sure that it is kept solely for this purpose. Look for the foods that give the best value for money. A cheap cut of meat is just as nutritious as the most expensive steak. With some thought and good cooking, it is easy to transform inexpensive foods into the most delicious dishes, and economy need not be apparent. To cook fresh food is much better value for money.

Shopping
A shopping list is important. It allows you to make certain that you have all you need, and makes it easier to estimate the amount you will spend. List foods needed for main meals, plus the fruit, eggs, groceries and so on that will be wanted in addition. Check your store cupboard to see if any stocks are getting low and need to be replaced. Renew stocks in turn, so that nothing is left to go stale.

Time
The length of time available to prepare and cook food makes all the difference to the type of meals you serve. But tasty, attractive and nutritious meals can be prepared, regardless of time. Busy people need to use quick methods of cooking, such as grilling, or plan to cook stews and casseroles which need little attention.

Food in season

Hot warming meals will be most in demand in winter and cool fresh salads in summer. The foods which are at their best and cheapest are always those in season, so use the charts of fish, vegetables and fruit for guidance. There are rarely any advantages in using out of season foods.

The kitchen

Plan to cook several dishes that can be cooked in the oven at the same time, remembering that in most ovens (except fan cookers) the heat is higher at the top than at the bottom. There is obviously considerable fuel economy in doing this. When entertaining a crowd, check that you have the cooking equipment and serving dishes necessary.

Colour, flavour and texture

Visual appeal is always a good stimulus to the appetite, so make food look neat, fresh and attractive. Choose foods for appearance as well as taste and plan menus with contrasting colours for instance, chicken in a cream sauce could be served with green beans and tomatoes. Colourful garnishes can be both attractive and nutritious.

Make sure that food always tastes as good as it smells. The only way to check that gravies, sauces, casseroles etc. taste good is to taste them yourself, and taste as you go along. Just a little on the tip of a teaspoon is enough to tell you whether more salt or pepper is wanted. Use a clean teaspoon for tasting and rinse it between tastes. Flavours taste better for contrast, so choose dishes that have different ingredients. For instance, avoid a mushroom soup followed by a beef and mushroom casserole, or a cheese flan with cauliflower cheese.

Use contrasting textures for appetizing food. Some foods are soft, others chewy and some crisp. For example, a poached fish dish could be followed by a crisp pastry flan.

The cook/hostess

There is an art in thinking out menus and cooking for your guests so that you can entertain them properly, too. You must allow some time to get ready for the party. When your guests arrive, you will want to be with them rather than in the kitchen. With this in mind, choose food which is easy to look after. A good choice would be a cold first course, a hot main course and then cold sweets. Only the hot main course will need attention and to be kept hot. Casseroles of all kinds can easily be kept hot. Grills and fried foods are difficult when entertaining, as the hostess spends too long in the kitchen with the last minute cooking.

Wine and food.

The use of wine in cooking enhances many dishes.

Which wine to use

Any wine can be used in cooking. Even if a recipe needs a special wine, you certainly don't have to use the most expensive. In general, it makes sense to use the same type of wine for cooking that you will be drinking with the dish.

A dry wine will usually blend better than a sweet one with savoury food. Sherry can be used in many savoury and sweet dishes, and a small amount of brandy or liqueur adds a little panache. Using cider and beer in cooking will also add character to many dishes. Dry cider can be used in place of white wine and many stews are excellent cooked with beer.

Add only a little wine to get a good flavour, most recipes need no more than 150–300 ml/$\frac{1}{4}$–$\frac{1}{2}$ pint.

Using leftover wine

If any wine is left in a bottle after a dinner or party, use it for cooking. Push the cork back firmly into the bottle neck and keep in a cool place. The wine will certainly still be fine to cook with in 1–2 weeks time. A bottle of cider lasts for ages if the top is screwed on tightly. It doesn't matter if it goes flat because the bubbles are not necessary. If cider or wine is not tightly stoppered, it becomes acid.

Soups

Add a little wine to soup just before serving. Flavour a clear consommé with dry sherry or Madeira. Add Italian vermouth to chicken or mushroom soup. A little sherry adds flavour to a creamy fish soup.

Fish and meat

Seafood cocktail is good with a little sherry in the mayonnaise. Use some white wine, vermouth or cider in the liquid when poaching fish. Make the cooking liquid into a sauce afterwards.

Not only does wine or beer taste good in a casserole, if the meat is marinaded in it overnight, it helps to tenderize as well. Red wine or beer with red meats, and white wine or cider with chicken, white meats and fish is the general rule. Some fish such as salmon or halibut, have a special flavour if cooked in red wine. Game can be cooked with either red or white wine, and port can be added to hare. When wine is added to a dish, it should always be boiled for a few minutes to drive off the alcohol.

Wine or cider can make a very quick sauce to serve with a roasted joint, fried meat or fish. When the food is cooked, keep it hot in the oven while preparing the sauce. Pour off all but 1–2 tablespoons fat from the pan and add a wineglass of wine or cider. Mix with the cooking juices and boil for 1–2 minutes to reduce and boil off the alcohol. Season and serve, or add a little cream to the sauce. Escalopes of veal cooked in this way with Marsala are a typical Italian dish.

Wine with puddings and desserts

So many simple desserts can be served by mixing fruit with a little wine or liqueur. Pineapple and Kirsch is well known, but strawberries in Marsala or port are equally delightful. Old English Trifle needs sherry and brandy added, although some people prefer port, and brandy or rum butter goes well with the Christmas pudding.

Stew raspberries and redcurrants or other soft fruits with a little red wine and sugar. Thicken the juice with arrowroot, then chill and serve with whipped cream and crisp biscuits.

Flambé dishes

In a restaurant flambé dishes, like crêpes Suzette, can be spectacular and the flavour is superb. The kitchen is probably a safer place to do this than the dining room, and here are a few rules to follow.

Don't have too much fat in the pan, pour it away if necessary.

Always measure the amount of brandy into a jug or small bowl. Then gently warm the brandy or liqueur in a pan, it will flame more easily.

Keep the flames well away from curtains, tea towels etc. A cover for your frying pan is a good idea, in case the flames get too high.

If you are serving a dish which needs flaming at the table, like Christmas pudding, always take the dish to the table with the brandy or liqueur in a jug. Pour a little brandy etc. over the dish and set light to it there. It may look exciting carrying a lighted Christmas pudding into a dark room, but there is a great danger of the flames sweeping back and burning you.

Dictionary of cookery terms.

Open any recipe book and you will find that there are a number of cookery terms used. This is a kind of cook's shorthand which quickly explains exactly how to work. The instruction to 'baste a joint' or 'cut into julienne strips' can sound rather off-putting unless you know what to do. This dictionary will tell you how to interpret them, so that you can follow recipes with ease.

Acid Lemon, vinegar, sour milk and soured cream are all sharp tasting acid foods which have special uses in cooking.
Aspic Transparent savoury jelly made from clarified meat or fish stock, used to garnish cold dishes.
Bain marie Water bath. Double saucepan or pan of hot water for keeping food hot, or for slow cooking.
Bake blind To bake empty tart and flan cases.
Barding To cover the breast of game or poultry with a piece of pork fat or bacon fat to keep it moist during roasting.
Basting To spoon fat and pan juices over food during baking in order to keep it moist and well flavoured.
Batter Flour, egg and liquid, beaten together to a semi-liquid mixture. Used to make pancakes, Yorkshire pudding, coating for fried food.
Beurre manié A mixture of half to two-thirds butter and flour worked together to a paste which is used to thicken sauces. It is whisked into the boiling liquid, then cooked for 3–4 minutes.
Blanching *a*) To pour boiling water over a food such as almonds, tomatoes or peaches in order to remove the skin. *b*) To cook in boiling water for a brief time e.g. before freezing.
Bouillon Stock or clear broth
Bouquet garni A bunch of herbs for flavouring food. This consists of parsley, thyme and bay leaf, sometimes with other herbs added.
Canapés Small savoury appetizers, often made from a bread or pastry base with a savoury topping and garnish.

Caramel Sugar boiled to a toffee brown colour; used for lining tins for puddings and flavouring milk. Can be poured on to an oiled tin, left to get cold and then broken up for topping desserts.

Chaudfroid A cold savoury sauce set with gelatine, used to give a white or brown coating to cold poultry, game and fish dishes.

Chine To saw through the base of rib and loin bones of meat, so that the backbone can easily be removed before or after cooking.

Clarify *a*) To remove impurities from dripping so that it can be used for frying or cake-making. Melt the fat, strain it, then put in a large bowl and pour over boiling water. Stir well and leave to cool and set. Lift off the layer of fat and warm it gently in a saucepan until the remaining water is driven off. Use immediately or leave in a bowl to set. *b*) To heat butter to remove salt and sediment. Heat gently in a pan until the water is driven off. Leave to settle, then pour off the fat, ready to use. *c*) To clear stock for consommé, aspic, or fruit juice for jellies. The stock is heated with egg whites which coagulate and collect all the impurities which are then strained off.

Coating To cover food with a layer of flour, egg and breadcrumbs or batter. Alternatively, covering food with a thin layer of sauce.

Cocottes Individual ovenproof dishes.

Concasser To chop roughly e.g. tomatoes.

Coral The red eggs (roe) of lobster or crab. This is often used to flavour and colour the sauce.

Cordon bleu A first class cook (traditionally a woman) or a high standard of cooking.

Court bouillon The flavoured liquid used for poaching food, especially fish. It contains water, or water and wine, flavoured with onion, carrot, bouquet garni and sometimes leek or celery. This is cooked for 20 minutes then allowed to cool before the uncooked food is added.

Creaming To beat sugar and butter together until light and fluffy, and of a consistency which will drop from the spoon.

Croquettes Savoury mixtures of cooked meat, poultry, fish or potato, coated in egg and breadcrumbs and deep fried.

Croûte A slice of fried or toasted bread on which food is served.

Croûtons Small dice of bread which are usually fried, but occasionally toasted, and served with soups.

Curdle A separated mixture may occur in sauces made from egg and butter or oil, and egg and milk mixtures such as egg custard.

Dariole A small mould with sloping sides, used for baking castle puddings or moulding jelly.

Dice To cut into small cubes.
Déglacer After shallow frying foods such as meat or fish, the pan drippings and some of the fat can be blended into a smooth sauce by the addition of liquid to the hot pan. Stock, wine, lemon juice or brandy are commonly used.
Dégorger *a*) To soak in cold water. *b*) To sprinkle with salt and allow to stand to withdraw liquid, e.g. when preparing aubergines, which are then rinsed and dried.
To dress *a*) To pluck, draw and truss poultry ready for cooking. *b*) To prepare crab or lobster meat.
Dressing The cold sauce used to moisten and add flavour to a salad.
Dripping Natural fats which melt from roasted meat or poultry while cooking.
Dropping consistency The texture at which a mixture will drop from a spoon when lightly tapped.
Duxelle A mixture of very fine chopped onion and mushrooms cooked with seasoning; often used as a savoury stuffing.
En croûte Meat, poultry or pâté cooked in a pastry case.
Escalopes Thin slices of lean, tender meat e.g. veal or turkey.
Faggot The old English term for a bunch of flavouring herbs.
Farce Stuffing.
To fillet To cut the flesh of fish or breast of poultry from the bones.
Fines herbes Chopped herbs mixed together, e.g. parsley, chives, chervil and tarragon. Sometimes parsley only is used.
Flamber To flame. Alcohol such as brandy or rum is poured over food and set fire to so that the alcohol is burnt off, leaving an aromatic flavour.
Flameproof A dish which is sufficiently heatproof to put directly on the top heat of the cooker.
Flan Pastry case – either sweet or savoury, or a specially shaped sponge base for a pudding.
Fold in To lightly blend flour, whipped cream, whisked egg whites etc. into a light mixture with a spatula or large spoon, using a folding motion so that the air is retained.
Fondant icing A soft, shiny, boiled sugar icing, mainly used by confectioners on buns and gâteaux.
Fritter Food coated in a batter and deep fried, or deep fried choux paste.
Frosting *a*) The edge of wine glasses or sundae glasses can be frosted by dipping first into lightly beaten egg white then into caster sugar. Leave to set before use. *b*) Some cake icings.

Frying Cooking food in hot fat – usually butter, lard, white cooking fat, dripping or oil.
Fumet Concentrated fish stock.
Garnish To decorate with edible foods to improve the appearance of a savoury dish.
Genoese A lightly whisked sponge with a little butter added to keep it moist.
Glacé Iced, or glazed with aspic.
Glaze To give a shiny surface to bread or pastry with beaten egg, or to cakes and flans with smooth boiling hot sieved jam or arrowroot glaze.
Gut To remove the entrails from fish.
Haute cuisine High class cooking.
Hang Meat, poultry and game are allowed to hang for a period of time in a cool atmosphere, to tenderize the meat and improve the flavour.
Hull To remove the stalk and centre core from soft fruit such as strawberries.
Icing Sugar confection used to decorate cakes.
Infuse To flavour hot liquid by soaking flavouring ingredients in it.
Julienne Matchstick like strips of vegetables, orange peel etc.
Knead To work a dough well together, as when making bread.
Kosher Foods prepared in accordance with Jewish Law.
Larding To insert strips of pork fat or fat bacon through meat using a special larding needle. Used to moisten lean meats during cooking.
Lardons The small strips of fat used for larding.
Liaison Thickening such as cream and egg yolks used in a sauce.
Lukewarm Just warm to touch at about blood heat.
Liquidize To put liquid, possibly with some solid ingredients, into a liquidizer or blender in order to purée it.
Macedoine A dice of fruit or vegetables.
Macerate To soak fruit in liqueur or other flavouring.
Marinade Liquid used to soak meat, game, poultry, fish etc. in order to flavour and tenderize it.
Marinate The process of soaking food in a marinade for a period of time before cooking it.
Meringue A light mixture of stiffly whisked egg whites with sugar which is cooked.
Mirepoix The mixture of bacon, onion, carrot and sometimes leek and celery which is used as the basis for a braise.
Noisette Butter cooked to a nut brown colour.
Offal The edible parts of an animal, other than the flesh, e.g. liver, kidneys, sweetbreads, tripe, brains, tongue, oxtail etc.

Parboil To part-boil, e.g. cooking potatoes for a few minutes in boiling water before roasting to help them to crisp in the oven.
Pâte French for pastry or dough.
Pith The bitter white part of the skin of citrus fruits.
Pluck To remove the feathers from poultry or game.
Poach To cook food gently in simmering liquid.
Pot roast A method of cooking meat in a tightly closed pan with some fat and a little liquid.
Praline Clear brown almond toffee which is crushed and used for flavouring and decoration.
Prove To allow a yeast dough to rise.
Purée A smoothly sieved mixture. The food to be puréed may be pressed through a sieve or blended in a liquidizer or food processor.
Reduce Boiling a liquid rapidly to concentrate the flavour.
Sauter Literally 'to jump'. A type of frying in which very hot fat is used and the food browned quickly in it.
Scald To heat a liquid to just below boiling point e.g. milk, when bubbles show round the edge of the pan.
Sear To brown quickly at a high temperature to seal the surface of meat.
To season To add salt and pepper.
Seasoned flour Flour mixed with salt and pepper.
Seasoning Salt, pepper, herbs and spices used to give flavour.
Simmer To keep liquid at just below boiling point.
Singe To burn the hairs off poultry or game.
Skim To remove scum from the top of boiling liquid.
Slake To blend with cold liquid.
Sorbet Water ice usually fruit flavoured.
Sousing Gentle cooking of fish in vinegar, spices and herbs.
Steaming The process of cooking food over steam.
Steep To soak.
Stock A well flavoured liquid made by boiling meaty bones with onion, carrot, bouquet garni etc. Used for soups, sauces and stews.
Strain To put through a sieve.
To sweat To cook food in a closed pan in its own steam and juices.
Syrup Sugar dissolved by heating in water.
Truss To tie or skewer poultry or game into shape before cooking.
Water bath See Bain marie.
Whip, whisk To beat air into light mixtures.
Zest The outside coloured layer of the skin of citrus fruit such as lemons.

Cook's time check.

To help the cook find the cooking time of almost any food, cooked by one of the many different methods, the information has been grouped together for easy reference in the following charts. In spite of all the controls on cookers today, the heat will vary from oven to oven. The temperatures given here provide a reasonable guide but do take the performance of your own oven into account.

Roasting is a traditional method of cooking in this country. Once, it was carried out on a spit over an open fire and, with present day cookers, spit roasting has again become fashionable. Microwave ovens are one of the latest technical advancements in modern cookery methods. For both these types of cooking, it is not possible to give definite times as they vary according to the make. However, a few notes on their use are included.

Spit roasting

Some gas and electric cookers are fitted with a spit which turns under the grill. With these, preheat the grill at high heat, secure the meat firmly on the spit and place in position. Make certain that it turns without obstruction and follow the manufacturer's instructions for heat control and time. If the spit is in the oven, use normal roasting times.

Meat for spit roasting must be a neat shape if it is to cook evenly, so make certain the poultry and meat are neatly trussed or tied. Awkward shaped joints, such as a shoulder of lamb or a loin of pork, should be boned first, then rolled and tied.

Microwave cooking

Microwave cooking is much faster than conventional methods. Microwave ovens work by bombarding the food with very short radiation waves which penetrate no more than 2.5 cm/1 inch. The waves agitate the molecules in the food and this produces the heat which cooks it.

If food is thicker than this, the inside is cooked by heat conducted from the hot outer layer. Each microwave oven model varies, so use the times given in the manufacturer's book.

Do not use metal, foil and dishes with a lead glaze or gold or silver decoration, as they reflect the waves and could damage the oven. Use and clean the oven according to the instruction book and have it checked once a year to make sure it is working safely.

ROASTING AND BAKING

Oven roasting

For oven roasting meat and some poultry, choose from either of these temperatures: 200°C, 400°F, Gas Mark 6 or 180°C, 350°F, Gas Mark 4. Roasting at a very high temperature produces meat which has an excellent flavour but there will be a lot of shrinkage. Also, only meat of prime quality can be cooked at a high temperature, other cuts will become dry and tough. At 200°C, 400°F, Gas Mark 6, the temperature is hot enough to brown the outside of the meat satisfactorily and still allow the inside to be cooked to the degree preferred, without drying out. Slow roasting at 180°C, 350°F, Gas Mark 4 will still produce meat with a brown outside. The lower heat enables medium quality joints of beef and small joints to retain their succulence and become tender to eat. There is less shrinkage, too. Large birds such as turkey and goose and most game are best slow roasted at 160°C, 325°F, Gas Mark 3.

All beef, lamb and veal can be roasted in the oven straight from the freezer, providing an oven thermometer is used. The disadvantage of meat cooked from frozen is that there can be as much as 50 per cent shrinkage.

It is essential that pork, poultry and game are completely defrosted before they are cooked, and other meats are possibly safer, too. Because the centre of the meat takes a long time to heat through when it is frozen, the long sustained warmth is conducive to the development of harmful bacteria.

For the best and tastiest results when roasting, preheat the oven, heat some fat, season the meat and sear the meat on all cut surfaces before cooking. Once the cooking has been completed, it is important to allow the joint to rest in a warm place for 10–15 minutes before carving.

Roasting bags are an up-to-date version of a covered roasting tin. The meat is partly cooked in the steam produced, so it is not a true method of roasting, but it helps to tenderize tough cuts of meat. Take care when opening the bag at the end of the cooking time as the hot fat and juices easily splash out. Roasting bags prevent fat splashing the oven and so keep it clean, but it is a matter of personal preference whether the cost is justified.

The delicate flesh of the breasts of poultry and large game such as pheasant should be protected by a light covering of foil or greaseproof paper to prevent them from becoming dry. This should be removed half an hour before the end of cooking time to enable the skin to brown. All roasting and baking times are for a preheated oven, with the shelf in position just above the centre of the oven. Weigh meat and poultry after stuffing and assess the cooking time from the total weight.

MEAT	200°C, 400°F, GAS MARK 6	180°C, 350°F, GAS MARK 4
Beef		
Up to 2.75 kg/6 lb		
All joints		
Rare	15 mins per 450 g/1 lb plus 15 mins	20 mins per 450 g/1 lb plus 20 mins
Medium	20 mins per 450 g/1 lb plus 20 mins	27 mins per 450 g/1 lb plus 27 mins
Well done	25 mins per 450 g/1 lb plus 25 mins	33 mins per 450 g/1 lb plus 33 mins
From 2.75–4.5 kg/ 6–10 lb		
Rare		
bone in	12 mins per 450 g/1 lb plus 12 mins	18 mins per 450 g/1 lb plus 18 mins
boneless	15 mins per 450 g/1 lb plus 15 mins	20 mins per 450 g/1 lb plus 20 mins
Medium		
bone in	15 mins per 450 g/1 lb plus 15 mins	20 mins per 450 g/1 lb plus 20 mins
boneless	18 mins per 450 g/1 lb plus 18 mins	25 mins per 450 g/1 lb plus 25 mins
Well done		
bone in	18 mins per 450 g/1 lb plus 18 mins	25 mins per 450 g/1 lb plus 25 mins
boneless	20 mins per 450 g/1 lb plus 20 mins	27 mins per 450 g/1 lb plus 27 mins

MEAT	200°C, 400°F, GAS MARK 6	180°C, 350°F, GAS MARK 4
Beef – contd.		
Over 4.5 kg/10 lb		
Rare		
bone in	10 mins per 450 g/1 lb plus 10 mins	15 mins per 450 g/1 lb plus 15 mins
boneless	12 mins per 450 g/1 lb plus 12 mins	18 mins per 450 g/1 lb plus 18 mins
Medium		
bone in	12 mins per 450 g/1 lb plus 12 mins	18 mins per 450 g/1 lb plus 18 mins
boneless	15 mins per 450 g/1 lb plus 15 mins	20 mins per 450 g/1 lb plus 20 mins
Well done		
bone in	15 mins per 450 g/1 lb plus 15 mins	20 mins per 450 g/1 lb plus 20 mins
boneless	18 mins per 450 g/1 lb plus 18 mins	25 mins per 450 g/1 lb plus 25 mins
Lamb		
Best end		
New Zealand	Not recommended	55 mins – 1 hour total cooking time
Home produced	Not recommended	1¼ hours total cooking time
Loin		
New Zealand	Not recommended	1¼–1¾ hours total cooking time
Home produced	Not recommended	1½–2 hours total cooking time
Other joints		
New Zealand	20 mins per 450 g/1 lb plus 20 mins	30 mins per 450 g/1 lb plus 30 mins
Home produced	20 mins per 450 g/1 lb plus 20 mins	30 mins per 450 g/1 lb plus 30 mins
Veal	25 mins per 450 g/1 lb plus 25 mins	35 mins per 450 g/1 lb plus 35 mins
Pork	30 mins per 450 g/1 lb plus 30 mins	40 mins per 450 g/1 lb plus 40 mins

Meat thermometer temperatures
Insert the thermometer in the meat about 30 minutes before the estimated end of the cooking time. Make certain the tip of the thermometer is in the centre of the thickest part of the meat and not against a bone.

	°C	°F
Beef		
Rare	60°	140°
Medium	71°	160°
Well done	79°	174°
Lamb		
Medium	77°	170°
Well done under 1.75 kg/4 lb	82°	180°
Well done over 1.75 kg/4 lb	79°	174°
Veal	75°	167°
Pork	88°	190°

BAKED BACON JOINTS, GAMMON AND HAM

All these joints need soaking in cold water to remove excess salt.
Soak smoked bacon up to 2.75 kg/6 lb overnight.
Soak smoked gammon and ham over 2.75 kg/6 lb 24 hours.
Soak green bacon up to 2.75 kg/6 lb 4 hours.
over 2.75 kg/6 lb 6–8 hours.
Cook, wrapped in foil, for total cooking time. Or boil for half the time, wrap in foil and finish cooking in the oven. Remove foil and glaze 30 minutes before the end of cooking time.

The following cooking times are the same for boiling.

	200°C, 400°F, Gas Mark 6
Up to 2.75 kg/6 lb (1 hour minimum cooking time)	20 mins per 450 g/1 lb plus 20 mins
2.75–4.5 kg/6–10 lb	18 mins per 450 g/1 lb plus 18 mins
4.5–6.75 kg/10–15 lb	15 mins per 450 g/1 lb plus 15 mins
6.75–9 kg/15–20 lb	12 mins per 450 g/1 lb plus 12 mins

OFFAL

	200°C, 400°F, GAS MARK 6	180°C, 350°F, GAS MARK 4
Hearts		
Stuffed lamb's	Not recommended	1¼–1¾ hours total cooking time
Stuffed calf's	Not recommended	2¼ hours total cooking time

POULTRY AND GAME

	200°C, 400°F, GAS MARK6	180°C, 350°F, GAS MARK 4 or 160°C, 325°F, GAS MARK 3 (*Indicated by italic type*)
* If body cavity is stuffed, allow another 20–30 mins total cooking time.		
Petit poussin	40–45 mins	1–1¼ hours total cooking time
*Chicken (stuffed neck end only)	20 mins per 450 g/1 lb plus 20 mins	25 mins per 450 g/1 lb plus 25 mins
*Capon 3.5 kg/8 lb	15 mins per 450 g/1 lb plus 15 mins	20 mins per 450 g/1 lb plus 20 mins
*Turkey Cover top of bird loosely with foil		
Up to 4.5 kg/10 lb	20 mins per 450 g/1 lb plus 20 mins	*20 mins per 450 g/1 lb plus 30 mins*
4.5–6.75 kg/10–15 lb	18 mins per 450 g/1 lb plus 18 mins	*25 mins per 450 g/1 lb plus 25 mins*
6.75–9 kg/15–20 lb	15 mins per 450 g/1 lb plus 15 mins	*20 mins per 450 g/1 lb plus 20 mins*
Over 9 kg/20 lb	12 mins per 450 g/1 lb plus 12 mins	*18 mins per 450 g/1 lb plus 18 mins*
Duckling	20 mins per 450 g/1 lb plus 20 mins	30–35 mins per 450 g/1 lb plus 30–35 mins
Duck	20 mins per 450 g/1 lb plus 20 mins	30–35 mins per 450 g/1 lb plus 30–35 mins
Goose		
about 4.5 kg/10 lb	Not recommended	*3 hours total cooking time*
about 6.75 kg/15 lb	Not recommended	*4 hours total cooking time*

	200°C, 400°F, GAS MARK 6	**180°C, 350°F, GAS MARK 4 or 160°C, 325°F, GAS MARK 3** (*Indicated by italic type*)
Guinea fowl	1–1¼ hours total cooking time	*1½–1¾ hours total cooking time*
Pheasant	45 mins–1 hour total cooking time	*1¼–1½ hours total cooking time*
Partridge	35–50 mins total cooking time	*45 mins–1 hour 5 mins total cooking time*
Grouse	30–35 mins total cooking time	*40 mins–1 hour total cooking time*
Teal	35 mins total cooking time	*45 mins total cooking time*
Mallard	30–40 mins total cooking time	*40–50 mins total cooking time*
Pigeon	20–25 mins total cooking time	*35–45 mins total cooking time*
Rabbit	about 1 hour total cooking time	*1¼–1½ hours total cooking time*
Venison		
In a flour and water paste	Not recommended	40 mins per 450 g/1 lb plus 40 mins
Covered in foil	Not recommended	25 mins per 450 g/1 lb plus 25 mins

FISH	**°C**	**°F**	**GAS MARK**	
Covered with greaseproof paper or wrapped in foil.				
Thin fillets	190	375	5	15–20 mins total cooking time
Thick fillets, cutlets, steaks	190	375	5	20–30 mins total cooking time
Small whole fish	190	375	5	20–30 mins total cooking time
Salmon				
up to 2.25 kg/5 lb	200	400	6	15 mins per 450 g/1 lb
up to 3.5 kg/8 lb	200	400	6	12 mins per 450 g/1 lb
over 3.5 kg/8 lb	200	400	6	10 mins per 450 g/1 lb
Stuffed whole fish, e.g. plaice, salmon, trout				
1 kg/2 lb	190	375	5	25–30 mins total cooking time
2 kg/4½ lb (weigh when stuffed)	190	375	5	45 mins total cooking time

VEGETABLES	°C	°F	GAS MARK	
Stuffed Spanish onions	200	400	6	Parboil 20 mins, then stuff and bake for further 1–1½ hours.
Parsnips	200	400	6	Parboil 5 mins. Roast 1 hour.
Potatoes				
Jacket	200	400	6	1–1½ hours
Roast	200	400	6	Parboil 5 mins. Roast 1¼–1½ hours.
Stuffed green peppers	200	400	6	Parboil 5–10 mins. Stuff and bake for further 45–50 mins.
Stuffed marrow rings	200	400	6	Boil 6–7 mins. Stuff and bake 30–40 mins.
Tomato				
Halves	180	350	4	5–10 mins
Medium whole	180	350	4	15 mins

PASTRY				
Meat pie with flaky pastry and cooked filling	220 180	425 350	7 then 4	20 mins. Then reduce temperature for further 20–25 mins.
Meat pies with flaky pastry and raw filling:	220	425	7 then	20 mins. Then cover pastry and reduce temperature:
Steak and kidney	160	325	3	for further 3–3½ hours
Veal and ham	160	325	3	further 1–1½ hours
Chicken	160	325	3	further 1–1½ hours.
Fruit pie with short-crust pastry	200 190	400 375	6 then 5	20 mins. Then reduce temperature until fruit is cooked.
Flan case (baked blind):				Remove beans and paper for last 5 mins.
Shortcrust pastry	200	400	6	20–25 mins
Flaky pastry	200–220	400–425	6–7	20–25 mins
Sweet shortcrust	190	375	5	25–30 mins
Puff pastry				
Vol-au-vent	220–230	425–450	7–8	30–35 mins

BISCUITS	°C	°F	GAS MARK	
Melting method				
Brandy snaps	180	350	4	15 mins
Flapjacks in tin size 20 × 30 cm/8 × 12 inch	190	375	5	30 mins
Shortbread – fingers	160	325	3	15 mins
– whole	160	325	3	1 hour
Creamed biscuits, e.g. Shrewsbury	160	325	3	25–30 mins
BREAD				
Bread rolls	220–230	425–450	7–8	10–15 mins
Loaves				
450 g/1 lb tin	220–230	425–450	7–8	30–40 mins
1 kg/2 lb tin				40–45 mins
CAKES				
Scones	230	450	8	7–10 mins
Rock cakes	190	375	5	15–20 mins
Gingerbread (depending on size)	160–180	325–350	3–4	45 mins–1¼ hours
Plain rubbed-in cake in 15 cm/6 inch tin	180	350	4	1¼ hours
Queen cakes				
flat tops	180	350	4	20 mins
peaked tops	200	400	6	15 mins
Victoria sandwich (3 egg mixture)	180	350	4	35–40 mins
Maderia cake (4 egg mixture)	160	325	3	1½ hours
Dundee cake in 20 cm/8 inch tin	150	300	2	3½ hours
Rich fruit cake in 18 cm/7 inch tin	140	275	1	3½–4 hours
Whisked sponge in 18 cm/7 inch tin (3 egg mixture)	180	350	4	25–30 mins
Swiss roll	220	425	7	7–8 mins
Meringues	120–140	250–275	½–1	2–3 hours

PUDDINGS	°C	°F	GAS MARK	
Yorkshire pudding				
large	220	425	7	30–40 mins
individual				15 mins
Rice	150	300	2	2–2½ hours
Tapioca	150	300	2	2–2½ hours
Sago	150	300	2	1½ hours
Baked egg custard	160	325	3	40–45 mins
Bread and butter pudding	180	350	4	30–40 mins
Baked apples	200	400	6	About 1 hour

GRILLING AND SHALLOW FRYING

In both cases seal the meat on both sides at a high temperature, then reduce the heat to medium to complete cooking. For a mixed grill, start with items needing the longest cooking time, then add others in turn.

	GRILLING – total time under a pre-heated grill	SHALLOW FRYING – total time
MEAT		
BEEF		
Steak 2–2.5 cm/¾–1 inch thick		
Rare	5 mins	5 mins
Medium rare	7–8 mins	7–8 mins
Well done	12 mins	12 mins
Minute steak 1 cm/½ inch thick	1–2 mins	1–2 mins
LAMB		
Chops 2–2.5 cm/¾–1 inch thick	10–15 mins	10–15 mins
Cutlets 2–2.5 cm/¾–1 inch thick	8–10 mins	8–10 mins
PORK		
Chops 2–2.5 cm/¾–1 inch thick	15–20 mins	20–25 mins
VEAL		
Escalopes	Not recommended	8–10 mins
Chops	Not recommended	15–20 mins

BACON		
Bacon rashers – thin	3–5 mins	3–5 mins
Gammon steaks 1 cm/½ inch thick	7–10 mins	7–10 mins
POULTRY		
Petit poussin (spatch cocked)	25–40 mins	Not recommended
Chicken, quarters	25–30 mins	Not recommended
Breasts	Not recommended	10–15 mins
OFFAL		
Kidney (cut in half), lamb's, pig's, veal	5–6 mins	5–6 mins
Liver, lamb's, pig's,	7–8 mins	7–8 mins
5 mm/¼ inch thick	5–6 mins	10–15 mins
SAUSAGES		
Large	15–20 mins	15–20 mins
Chipolatas	10–15 mins	10–15 mins
FISH		
Thin fillets	6–8 mins	5–12 mins
Thick fillets, cutlets, steaks no more than 2 cm/¾ inch thick	12–20 mins	12–15 mins
Whole fish		
Sprats	4–6 mins	5–6 mins
Trout, herring, mackerel	8–12 mins	12–15 mins
Sole, plaice	8–10 mins	10–12 mins
Kippers	5–6 mins	5–6 mins

DEEP FRYING

Most food to be deep fried must have a protective coating to prevent the fat penetrating it during cooking. Suitable coatings are given.

	SUITABLE COATINGS	°C	°F	
Meat				
Lamb cutlets, thin	Egg and breadcrumbs	185	370	5–6 mins
Pork steaks 1.5 cm/ ½ inch thick	Egg and breadcrumbs	180	360	7–8 mins

	SUITABLE COATINGS	°C	°F	
Poultry				
Chicken joints	Egg and breadcrumbs	170	350	15–20 mins
Chicken breasts	Egg and breadcrumbs	170	350	12–18 mins
Fish				
Whitebait	Flour	185	370	2–3 mins
Thin fillets	Egg and bread-crumbs or batter	185	370	5–8 mins
Steaks, cutlets, thick fillets no more than 2 cm/¾ inch thick	Egg and bread-crumbs or batter	185	370	8–10 mins
Whole sole, plaice	Egg and breadcrumbs	185	370	8–12 mins
Vegetables				
Artichokes, Jerusalem	Egg and breadcrumbs	180	360	Boil first for 15–20 mins. Drain well, coat and fry 4–5 mins
Aubergine fritters	Batter	185	370	4–5 mins
Courgettes	Egg and breadcrumbs	180	360	Cut into fingers. Blanch first in boiling salted water. Drain well, coat and fry 4–5 mins
Mushroom fritters	Egg and bread-crumbs or batter	185	370	4–5 mins
Onion rings, French fried	Dipped in milk and flour-coated	185	370	6–8 mins
Parsnips	Batter	185	370	Boil first 15–20 mins Drain well, coat and fry 4–5 mins

	SUITABLE COATINGS	°C	°F	
Potatoes				
Chips	—	160	320	5–6 mins until soft Remove from fat
		190	380	Then raise temperature and cook 3–4 mins until crisp and golden brown
Croquettes	Egg and breadcrumbs	185	370	10–15 mins
Game chips (crisps)	—	185	375	3–4 mins
Sweet fritters				
Apple (raw)	Batter	190	380	4–5 mins
Pineapple or banana	Batter	190	380	3–4 mins
Choux paste	—	170	350	5–7 mins
Other deep fried foods				
Chinese spring rolls	—	185	370	7–8 mins
Doughnuts	—	160	320	7–10 mins
Scotch eggs	Egg and breadcrumbs	170	350	12–15 mins

POACHING

180°C, 350°F, Gas Mark 4
or over low heat on top of cooker

FISH	
Fillets	15–20 mins
Cutlets	10 mins per 450 g/1 lb as a guide. 25 mins minimum time or allow 10 mins for each 2.5 cm/1 inch thickness
Trout	15–20 mins
Whole fish e.g. brill, turbot	30–45 mins depending on size

Poaching Cont.	**200°C, 400°F, Gas Mark 6 or over low heat on top of cooker**
Salmon	
Up to 2.25 kg/5 lb	15 mins per 450 g/1 lb
Up to 3.5 kg/8 lb	12 mins per 450 g/1 lb
Over 3.5 kg/8 lb	10 mins per 450 g/1 lb
	Top of cooker
POULTRY	
Chicken breasts (meat only – no bones)	7–10 mins. Start timing when liquid comes to simmering point. Don't overcook or they toughen.

STEWING OR POACHING FRUIT

	Over low heat on top of cooker in covered pan	**In oven in covered dish 160°C, 325°F, Gas Mark 3**
Apples (depends on type)		
Slices	10–15 mins	20–25 mins
Quarters	15–20 mins	35–45 mins
Purée	20–25 mins	Not recommended
Berries, Currants	5–15 mins	20–35 mins
Pears – whole or halved	20 mins –1½ hours	1–2 hours
Plums	10–20 mins	30–45 mins
Quinces	1½–2 hours	1½–2 hours
Rhubarb	7–10 mins	20–30 mins

BRAISING AND POT ROASTING

	160°C, 325°F, Gas Mark 3 or over low heat on top of cooker
MEAT	Brown meat and poultry first in hot fat.
Beef	45 mins per 450 g/1 lb plus 45 mins 2½–3 hours minimum cooking time
Lamb	30 mins per 450 g/1 lb plus 30 mins 1½–2 hours minimum cooking time

	160°C, 325°F, Gas Mark 3 or over low heat on top of cooker
Veal	40 mins per 450 g/1 lb plus 40 mins 1½–2 hours minimum cooking time
Pork	45 mins per 450 g/1 lb plus 45 mins 1¾–2¼ hours minimum cooking time
POULTRY AND GAME	
Chicken 1.5–1.75 kg/3–4 lb	1½–1¾ hours total cooking time
Duck	1¾–2½ hours total cooking time
Guinea fowl	40–45 mins total cooking time
Pheasant (depending on size)	
old	1½–2 hours total cooking time
young	45 mins–1 hour total cooking time
Partridge (depending on size and age)	2 hours total cooking time
Grouse (depending on size and age)	1½–2 hours total cooking time
Mallard (depending on size and age)	1½–2 hours total cooking time
Pigeon (depending on size and age)	1–1½ hours total cooking time
Rabbit (depending on size and age)	1–1½ hours total cooking time
Hare (depending on size and age)	
Saddle	1–1½ hours total cooking time
Remainder jointed	3 hours total cooking time
Venison 1.25–1.5 kg/2½–3½ lb	2½–3 hours total cooking time
OFFAL (braise only)	
Whole liver	
Lamb	1 hour minimum cooking time
Pork	1 hour minimum cooking time
Sliced ox liver	1 hour minimum cooking time
Hearts	
Lamb	1½–1¾ hours total cooking time
Pork, veal	2–2¼ hours total cooking time
Sliced ox	2 hours minimum cooking time
Tongues	
Lamb	Boil ½ hour, then braise 2 hours
Ox	Boil 2 hours, then braise 2 hours

	180°C, 350°F, Gas Mark 4
FISH (braising only)	10 mins per 450 g/1 lb. 25 mins minimum cooking time or allow 10 mins for each 2.5 cm/1 inch of thickness.
VEGETABLES (braising only)	
Carrots (small whole or quartered large)	1–1½ hours
Celery (short lengths)	Parboil 5 mins. Braise 1–1½ hours
Cabbage (quartered)	Parboil 5 mins. Braise 1–1½ hours
Fennel (small whole or quartered large)	Parboil 10 mins. Braise 1½–1¾ hours
Lettuce (quartered)	Parboil 2–3 mins. Braise 40–45 mins
Onions – small	Parboil 5 mins. Braise 40–45 mins
– large	Parboil 20 mins. Braise 1½–2 hours
	200°C, 400°F, Gas Mark 6
Chicory	Parboil 5–7 mins. Braise 30 mins
Leeks	Parboil 5 mins. Braise 1 hour

STEWS AND CASSEROLES

	160°C, 325°F, Gas Mark 3 or over low heat on top of cooker
MEAT	Total cooking time
Beef	
Chuck, blade-bone	2½–3 hours
Shin, neck, flank	3–4 hours
Pork	
Spare rib, blade-bone, hand and spring, belly	1¾–2½ hours
Chops	35–40 mins
Lamb (all cuts)	1½–2 hours
Veal	
Shoulder, breast, knuckle	1¼–1½ hours
POULTRY AND GAME	
Chicken	
Jointed roaster	45 mins–1 hour
Whole boiler	30 mins per 450 g/1 lb

	160°C, 325°F, Gas Mark 3 or over low heat on top of cooker
Rabbit – jointed	1½–2 hours
Hare – jugged	2½–3 hours
Pheasant – young	45 mins–1 hour
– old	1½–2 hours
Partridge	1½–2 hours
Venison	2½–3 hours
OFFAL	
Sweetbreads	
Calf's	1½–2 hours
Lamb's	1 hour
Tripe – prepared	1–1½ hours
Ox liver	1 hour minimum cooking time
kidney	1 hour minimum cooking time
Oxtail	3–4 hours

BOILING

Start timing when liquid comes to boiling point, then simmer.

MEAT	
Beef	
Fresh	20 mins per 450 g/1 lb plus 20 mins 1¼ hours minimum cooking time
Salt	30 mins per 450 g/1 lb plus 30 mins 1½ hours minimum cooking time
Lamb	20 mins per 450 g/1 lb plus 20 mins 1¼ hours minimum cooking time
Pork	
Fresh	20 mins per 450 g/1 lb plus 20 mins 1¼ hours minimum cooking time
Salt	25 mins per 450 g/1 lb plus 25 mins 1½ hours minimum cooking time
BACON JOINTS, HAM, GAMMON	See soaking and cooking times under baked bacon (page 169)
POULTRY	
Chicken	
Roaster	45 mins–1 hour total cooking time
Boiling fowl	2–4 hours

OFFAL	Total cooking time
Tongue	
Ox	$3\frac{1}{2}$–$4\frac{1}{2}$ hours
Lamb	$1\frac{1}{2}$ hours minimum cooking time
Calf	$1\frac{1}{2}$–2 hours

VEGETABLES	Total cooking time
Artichokes	
Globe	20–40 mins
Jerusalem	20–30 mins
Asparagus (tied in bundles)	15–25 mins
Beetroot	1–2 hours
Beans	
Broad	15–25 mins
French	15–20 mins
Runner (sliced)	15–25 mins
Bean sprouts	$\frac{1}{2}$–1 min
Broccoli – purple sprouting	10–15 mins
Brussels sprouts	10–15 mins
Cabbage	10–15 mins
Carrots – small whole or quartered large	15–20 mins
Cauliflower	15–20 mins
Chinese leaves	4–5 mins
Curly kale	15–20 mins
Celeriac – diced	30–35 mins
Celery – cut into short lengths	30–45 mins
Chicory – whole	30–40 mins
Courgettes – sliced	10–12 mins
Cucumber (cut into thick slices)	15–20 mins
Kohlrabi	20–30 mins
Leeks (depending on size)	20–30 mins
Marrow – cut into chunks	15–20 mins
Onions – small or sliced	20–30 mins
Parsnips – cut into chunks	20–30 mins
Peas	10–15 mins
Potatoes	
New	10–20 mins
Old	15–25 mins
Seakale	30–40 mins
Salsify	40–45 mins
Spinach	7–10 mins
Turnips – small whole or diced large	20–30 mins

DRIED VEGETABLES

Dried vegetables are used in the national dishes of almost every country – red kidney beans in a chilli con carne, chick peas in couscous, lentils in the golden yellow daal served with curry. They are made into vegetable dishes or soups, or they are added to meat and poultry dishes. All except red lentils need to be soaked overnight before cooking.

Do not put dried vegetables into salted water as the salt will harden them. Instead, add salt to the boiling vegetables 15 minutes before the end of the cooking time. Cooking times depend on the age of the dried vegetables. If they have been in stock for a long time they may take longer to cook.

Beans (soak overnight)	
Aduki	45 mins–1 hour
Borlotti	1–1¼ hours
Blackeyed	45 mins–1 hour
Butter	1½–2 hours
Dutch brown	1½–2 hours
Field	45 mins–1 hour
Flageolets	1–1¼ hours
Haricot	1½–2 hours
Pinto	1–1¼ hours
Red	2–2½ hours
Peas (soak overnight)	
Chick	1¾–2 hours
Dried	1½–1¾ hours
Split	1–1¼ hours
Lentils	
Brown (soak overnight)	40–50 mins
Orange (no need to soak)	30–40 mins
Pearl barley (no need to soak)	1½–1¾ hours

RICE AND DRIED PASTA

White rice	12–15 mins
Easy to cook rice	20 mins
Brown rice	30–40 mins
Quick macaroni	7–10 mins
Macaroni	18–20 mins
Pasta shells	15–20 mins
Noodles (tagliatelle)	10–12 mins
Lasagne	10–12 mins
Spaghetti	10–12 mins

STEAMING

FISH	
Thin fillets (on a plate)	10–15 mins
Cutlets, no more than 2 cm/ ¾ inch thick	15–20 mins
Salmon cutlets 2 cm/¾ inch thick, wrapped in foil	25–35 mins
Larger pieces of white fish wrapped in foil	15 mins per 450 g/1 lb plus 15 mins
Larger pieces of salmon wrapped in foil	20 mins per 450 g/1 lb plus 20 mins
Poultry	Steam for half as long again as normal boiling time
Vegetables	Steam for half as long again as normal boiling time.
MEAT PUDDINGS	
Steak and kidney pudding	3½–4 hours
Bacon roly-poly (longer cooking if raw onion is used)	2–2½ hours
SWEET PUDDINGS	
Jam roly-poly	2–2½ hours
Fruit pudding with suet pastry	1½–2 hours
Suet sponge pudding with syrup or raisins, etc.	2–2½ hours
Creamed sponge pudding	1–2 hours
Christmas pudding	8 hours. (Cooking time can be split. Minimum preliminary cooking time 4 hours.)

Weights and measures

These days, most recipes give quantities in both Metric and Imperial, that is pounds and pints, and kilograms and litres. It does not make any difference to your cooking which measures you use, but remember to use either metric or imperial quantities. They must not be mixed because the slight differences in the measures can cause problems. For instance, mixtures can become too thick or too thin etc.

SOLID INGREDIENTS

WEIGHT

Imperial

lb – pound; oz – ounce; 16 oz – 1 lb

Metric

kg – kilogram; g – gram; 1000 g – 1 kg

Weights used in recipes (approximate equivalents):

15 g	½ oz	225 g	8 oz
25 g	1 oz	350 g	12 oz
50 g	2 oz	450 g	1 lb
100 g	4 oz	500 g	1¼ lb
175 g	6 oz	1 kilogram	2–2¼ lb

LIQUID INGREDIENTS

LIQUID MEASURE

Imperial

fl oz – fluid ounce 20 fl oz – 1 pint

Metric

ml – millilitre 1000 ml – 1 litre

Measuring spoons (level)

2.5 ml – ½ teaspoon
5 ml – 1 teaspoon
15 ml – 1 tablespoon

Liquid measures used in recipes (approximate equivalents)

150 ml – ¼ pint	750 ml – 1¼ pints
300 ml – ½ pint	900 ml – 1½ pints
450 ml – ¾ pint	1 litre – 1¾ pints
600 ml – 1 pint	

AMERICAN CUPS

American cookery is based on measurement by volume. When the United States separated from Great Britain in the 18th century, the standard British size pint was 16 fluid ounces; it is now 20 fluid ounces.

This 16 fluid ounce measure became the kitchen measuring standard for their cooking with an 8 fluid ounce cup used as the measure, allowing two to the pint. You can buy cup measures with ¾, ½ and ¼ cups in a set. Metric cups of 250 ml are in use in Canada, New Zealand and Australia.

1 cup – 8 fluid ounces – 250 ml
1 cup holds 125 g flour, 225 g sugar and 225 g fat.

OVEN TEMPERATURES

	ELECTRICITY		GAS MARK
	degrees Celsius °C*	degrees Fahrenheit °F	
Very cool	110	225	¼
	120	250	½
Cool	140	275	1
	150	300	2
Moderate	160	325	3
	180	350	4
Moderately hot	190	375	5
	200	400	6
Hot	220	425	7
	230	450	8
Very hot	240	475	9

*to the nearest 10°C

Index

A

B

C

ACKNOWLEDGEMENTS The publishers and authors would like to thank the following for their help in compiling this book: Agrexco; Anne Dare of MEAT; Apple and Pear Development Council; Barbara Coyle of Fruit Trades Journal; British Butter Council; British Egg Council; British Farm Produce Council; British Sugar Bureau; Communicable Diseases Surveillance Centre; DHSS Catering and Dietetics Branch, Environmental Health Office; Dr. Louise Davis, Queen Elizabeth College; Dutch Dairy Bureau; Flour Advisory Bureau; Food Manufacturers Association; Food from France; Fresh Fruit and Vegetable Bureau; Game Conservancy; Gerald Watkins, Chief Inspector, Billingsgate Market; Jill Service for New Zealand Lamb; Mattessons; Metal Box Company; Milk Marketing Boards for England and Wales, Scotland, and Northern Ireland; The Food Manufacturers Research Association; The Other Sausage Bureau; White Fish Authority; and the many other contributors who kindly supplied information.